"Highly readable, intimate, and unpretentious, *The Way of Marriage* contains the complete answer. I recommend it enthusiastically to any couple."

Hugh and Gayle Prather
authors of *A Book for Couples*
and *Notes to Each Other*

THE WAY OF
MARRIAGE

THE WAY OF MARRIAGE

A Journal of Spiritual Growth through Conflict, Love, and Sex

HENRY JAMES BORYS

HarperSanFrancisco
A Division of HarperCollins*Publishers*

For information about speaking engagements
and seminars by Henry J. Borys,
please write 12756 103rd Place, NE; Kirkland, WA, 98034.

FIRST HARPERCOLLINS EDITION PUBLISHED IN 1993

Library of Congress Cataloging-in-Publication Data
Borys, Henry James
    The way of marriage : a journal of spiritual growth through
conflict, love, and sex / Henry James Borys.
        p. cm.
    Originally published : Kirkland, WA : Purna Press, ©1991.
    ISBN 0-06-250211-5
    1. Marriage. 2. Intimacy (Psychology). 3. Love. 4. Interpersonal relations. I. Title.
HQ734.B7412 1993
306.81—dc20   92–56411
                                                                          CIP

93   94   95   96   97 CWI   10 9 8 7 6 5 4 3 2 1

To Susan,
who fills me with her love and quiet wisdom,
whose pulse has become my own.

Contents

IV. THE INNER DANCE

V. A COMMUNION OF FEELING

VI. THE OTHER FACE OF LOVE

VII. ANGER: THE PHILOSOPHER'S STONE

VIII. BLOCKADING GROWTH

IX. THE PATH OF PERSONAL SEX

X. FINAL NOTE

Introduction

In the summer of 1985, my wife and I faced the single greatest challenge of our relationship. Through our efforts to meet that challenge, not only did we eventually rescue our marriage, but we discovered first-hand that marriage is a powerful path—one intricately designed to deepen and fulfill both partners. *The Way of Marriage*, based on my personal journal, is the story of our travels on that path.

In Lao Tsu's *Tao Te Ching*, or *Way of Life* (from which the title of this book is borrowed), "the way" refers not only to the path to perfection, but also to the goal: human life in a state of wholeness, in a state of perfect balance with the cosmos. No such claim can be made of *The Way of Marriage*. I make no pretense of describing a perfect marriage. If anything, it may seem to the reader that Susan and I proceed from one marital predicament to the next.

This is because it was in times of challenge that I felt most drawn to self-examination and to writing in my journal to sort through my feelings. Those were moments, not just of figuring something out or of writing about what I already knew, but of true discovery and growth. Those were moments when we encountered the greatest personal meaning, and it was then that we most clearly saw the reality of marriage as a path.

Yet even with all we have been through, our marriage has been filled with far more joy and love than conflict. Especially in recent years, we have enjoyed a depth of love and unity we could have only wished for when we first married. Though the reader may have to find some of this between the lines, I hope I have conveyed the joy, as well as the challenge, of this path.

Some may wonder why I have called this book "A Journal of *Spiritual* Growth." Certainly the tone of the book is not overtly religious. For the most part the book describes working through every-day, down-to-earth marital challenges. Why not simply call it "A Journal of *Personal* Growth"?

To us the distinction seems significant. Personal growth relates specifically to the individual. Although it can also relate to an individual's relationship with others, personal growth does not necessarily imply an evolving subjective relationship between the individual and life as a whole. Spiritual growth, however, does imply this.

Personal growth becomes *spiritual* growth when we see and feel that events in our lives relate to a meaning and intelligence beyond ourselves, yet intimately related to ourselves. Then as we meet our challenges to grow, we not only grow as individuals, we grow in our relationship with life. We begin to feel a personal connection with something higher and wiser than our own small egos.

14

It is in this broadest sense that I have used the term *spiritual growth*. Such spirituality may appear to be only in the eyes of the beholder, but in our eyes at least, our journey together has been a spiritual unfolding.

In transforming my journal into book form, much editing has taken place. Most significant, I have arranged the book into chapters by theme, rather than preserve the chronology of my journal. Though less organic, I hope this makes it more convenient to use this book as a reference—to refer to specific areas of interest as the reader faces challenges in his or her own relationship. I have also changed the names of friends mentioned in the book, out of respect for their privacy.

Finally, I realize that I have not offered anything close to a comprehensive picture of the way of marriage. For one thing, I have not even touched upon how our children have affected our marriage. For another, our journey is far from over; we are learning new lessons every day. But even more so, this book remains incomplete because every couple's journey on the way of marriage is uniquely their own. There may be patterns and principles we can learn from each other, but there are no pat formulas. Each couple will discover their way for themselves. If I have given enough of a glimpse of the way of marriage to show that it is a way, then I shall feel fortunate.

CHAPTER I

Turning Point

Before the Beginning

Seldom or never does a marriage develop into an individual relationship smoothly and without crisis. There is no birth of consciousness without pain.

—C. G. Jung

"I know I love you. I just can't feel it."

Having said this, I reached over to Susan's side of the bed to touch her arm, but she pulled away. She was crying. Folding my hands on my chest, I stared into the darkness of our bedroom and tried to think of something to say that would make her feel better.

"Don't cry, Susan. I love you. I just must be going through a phase or something."

This seemed to help because she stopped crying and blew her nose.

"I wasn't crying because of that," she said after a moment. "I was crying because I feel the same way; I don't feel my love for you either."

"Oh."

We had been married almost seven years. We'd had more than our share of fights. We had even separated twice. But at least we had always felt something for each other. This was the worst yet: no feeling.

We both lay still on opposite sides of our king-size bed. Only the sound of an occasional car passing by filled the void between us. I wondered how we could resolve things before going to sleep. But then what was there to resolve? Neither of us felt anything, and neither of us wanted to. Well, at least we could be civil.

"Good night, Susan."

"Good night, Henry," she replied softly.

Then without another word, we rolled onto our sides, facing away from each other, and went to sleep.

The next morning I left on a three-week sales trip covering five Western states. Ordinarily, the idea of driving for days alone, eating restaurant food, and sleeping in stale motel rooms was anything but inviting. This time, however, I relished the prospect of having some time and space to myself. In fact, although I usually called Susan every night when I was on a trip, for the first few days of this trip I did not call her once. When I finally called her on the fifth night I was met with some unexpected news.

An old friend of ours, David, had just arrived in Seattle and had asked Susan if we could put him up while he looked for an apartment. Susan had told him she would check with me. We had a spare room. David was in need. What could I say but yes? I didn't like the idea, but I had no reason not to trust Susan, even alone with a single man in the house. If Susan was anything she was true blue.

From then on I called Susan every night. After all, why worry her? But soon I was the one who began to worry, for with each passing day, Susan's voice grew inexplicably happier and lighter. Was our marital crisis simply dissolving away by itself? Unlikely.

I had been on the road for over two weeks, when one night I decided to put my fears to rest. I dialed Susan from my motel room. We talked for a few minutes. Finally, in a light-hearted tone I asked her.

"You and David aren't getting too friendly, are you?"

"Of course not," she reassured me. "We're having some wonderful talks, but don't worry, David is not my type."

"I know."

"Well, I have to go. David has dinner on."

"OK. Bye, I love you, Susan."

"Bye, Henry."

I slowly put the receiver back on its hook. David has dinner on? I could not remember cooking a meal for Susan our entire marriage. Now I *knew* I had to get home immediately, but I still had four more days on the road!

That night I hardly slept. The next morning I made two distracted sales calls but by lunch could not take it anymore. I dialed Susan's work number from a pay phone. When she answered I got right to the point.

"Susan, is anything going on between you and David?"

She hesitated.

"I told you last night not to worry," she said finally. "We'll talk about it when you get home."

"What do you mean we'll talk about it when I get home? If nothing's happening, what do we have to talk about?"

"Just don't worry, Henry. Look, I've got to go; this is our rush hour. You'll be home in a few days; we can talk then. Or call me tonight if you want, OK?"

"Bye," I said as if it were a swear word and slammed the phone on its hook.

This was worse than I thought. She knew that I knew what they were up to, but all she could say was that she had to get back to work! I felt incensed, crushed, and humiliated. Yet there was nothing I could do about it; I was still 1,200 miles from home.

The next two days were a blur of hurried sales and meteoric driving. I did not call Susan again. I hardly slept. All I could think of was getting back to confront them; my mind whirled with one scathing rebuke after another.

I had been scheduled to return home Friday afternoon, but it was just after eight o'clock on Thursday night when I pulled into our apartment parking stall. By this time I had decided that nothing I could say, no matter how scathing, would be enough. I would walk in on them, let their guilt speak for itself, then walk out. Forever.

I climbed the steps to our apartment and opened the door. Susan was washing dishes in the kitchen—alone. Her short sandy hair was pulled back, and her face was flushed with the heat of kitchen work. She looked up as I walked in.

"Henry, you're back!"

She dried her hands with a dishtowel, but did not make a move to give me the usual welcome home hug. We just stood there, facing each other.

"Where's David?" I asked. My voice sounded overly husky.

"He's gone," she replied. "He found an apartment and moved out two days ago."

I waited for more. Nothing came.

"Maybe we should sit down and talk," she said finally.

"Yeah. Maybe we should."

Without waiting for her, I walked into the living room and sat down on the couch. She followed and sat beside me.

"I'm sorry I couldn't talk to you at work the other day," she began, putting her hand on my arm.

I pulled away.

"I know you're upset," she continued, "but it's not what you think between David and me."

"Oh no? What is it then?"

"I'm not sure, but David and I are not lovers."

"Right. You've just been giving him cooking lessons."

"I'm telling the truth. We've never even kissed."

I looked into her eyes. She returned my look: unflinching, sincere. Susan could never lie this well. Then it hit me: she was telling the truth! At this a huge wave of relief swept over me. Thank God. If they had gone to bed together I couldn't have taken it. Maybe this was not going to be so bad after all.

"But I do feel something for David that I haven't felt in a long time," she continued, as tears filled her eyes. "I don't want to be attracted to David. It makes such a mess of things, because I *know* I still love you. But it's just happening. I don't know why, it just is."

As suddenly as it had come, my relief vanished.

"What are you saying? You love David?" I asked in a sarcastic tone, ignoring her tears.

"I don't think I . . . I don't know."

"What about your commitment to me?" I demanded. "We're married, remember?"

"You don't understand," Susan replied softly.

"I understand that you're being totally irresponsible. Would you risk our marriage for this thing with David? David is a klutz!"

"But you know what?" she asked.

"What?"

"David nurtures me in ways that I always wanted from you. He gives to me. He loves me, respects me, treats me like a woman. I've realized that . . . "

She paused. I could feel her reluctance to hurt my feelings.

"I've realized," she began again, looking down at her hands, "that I'd given up ever having that with you long ago."

"Oh give me a break," I said as if disgusted. Inwardly, though, I felt an uncomfortable pressure of truth in what she was saying. I knew that I had been self-centered—we'd had a million arguments about it—but hadn't I loved her?

She leaned toward me, her face tear-stained.

"I don't want to feel this for David, believe me," she said, pleading for my understanding. "I don't want to. But I do, and I haven't been able to just turn it off."

"Well just stop seeing him," I said matter-of-factly.

"You want me to just close the door on my feelings for David?"

"That's right. You would if you were committed to our marriage."

"I can't," she said, shaking her head slightly. "I can't do it, Henry, but even if I could, what about you and me then? What would have changed?"

We were both quiet. Part of me wanted to shake her: I could not believe she would throw away everything we had together. Yet another part of me knew that I had helped create this problem. For most of our marriage, I had demanded that she do the giving, the growing, to accommodate me. I had not made much effort to accommodate her at all.

"So I should just close the door on my feelings for David?" she asked again softly. "Is that what you really think?"

I wanted to say yes. I wanted to demand she stop seeing David. But I had to admit, what would we have then? I could not twist her arm to make her love me. I could not stop her from being attracted to David. It went against everything I wanted, against everything I believed marriage was about, but in that moment I felt I had no choice.

"No," I heard myself say, "I guess you can't ignore your feelings for David just for my sake."

I hoped she would contradict me. I hoped she would say that really she did love me. But she did not. She did not say anything.

I could not remember crying our entire relationship, but I felt like crying then. Instead, I stood up, brought my things into the spare bedroom, and closed the door.

*

During the next few weeks, Susan continued to see David. She said that she just could not turn her back on a friend, especially on a friend who made her feel cared for, attractive, and worthwhile as a person. She did promise that she would not become physically involved with him.

This put me in limbo. If Susan had been having a full-fledged affair, I would have walked out, but she was not; supposedly she still wanted our marriage to work. I could not take being in limbo. I reacted. I argued again and again that Susan should recommit to our marriage, that only this would solve our problems. But it was clear I was just reacting. A week passed before I realized that the only way I could avoid being cast as the jealous, raging husband was to keep quiet, and to do my best to let Susan go—without blame, without reaction, without possessiveness.

Ironically, I also found that I could not even make amends for my years of selfishness. When I tried now to give to her in ways that I had neglected over the years—making dinner, vacuuming, even just starting a conversation—I came across as pitifully solicitous. If I was not to be cast as the desperate husband, eagerly trying to win his wife back, again I had to let her go.

Now all the pain that I had never wanted to feel in my life came crashing down on me: the pain of facing that I was imperfect, small, and selfish; the pain of knowing that the attraction Susan could not feel for me, she felt for another man; worst of all, the pain that I might lose her. Yet as the days passed, I found that this pain did not destroy me as I had expected. Instead, I actually began to feel something humbling, almost sweet, within this pain. As if my pain were pushing me into a depth of feeling, even a dignity, that I had never felt before.

Sometimes, even when I knew Susan and David were together, I would feel this sense of depth and dignity. At those times I knew I could let Susan go completely if that was what she wanted. I had often heard people use the words "finding myself," but this had meant little to me. Now my heart was breaking open, and for the first time, I felt I might be finding myself.

It was during this period that I began to keep a journal. I had always wanted to keep one, but never had the discipline. Now it became a necessity. Nothing kept me in touch with myself like those few minutes spent writing my thoughts. I could be on the edge of jealousy or anger, but once I picked up my notebook, a part of me would instinctively seek the constructive meaning in what I was going through.

And so after seven years of marriage, in this search for constructive meaning, I finally took my first few steps on the way of marriage.

CHAPTER II

Breaking the Stone

Gifts of Pain

Love of God is pure when joy and suffering inspire an equal degree of gratitude.

—Simone Weil

A few days ago I discovered that Susan had taken David to Twin Falls (one of our favorite spots in the Cascade Mountains) for an afternoon. To me this seemed entirely irresponsible. I felt she should have more commitment to our marriage than that, or tell me what she is really feeling for David.

Anyway, I blew up and confronted her with it. Susan said that she and David just had a friendly afternoon. I asked her why they could not be friends here. Why did they have to go to the mountains? She said it did not matter where they were, David made her feel more appreciated and respected than she had felt with me for years. What could I say to that? For two days afterward we hardly spoke to each other.

Then yesterday I had the feeling that Susan had seen David again. I could not help myself; I started to pry. She said that she and David had met for lunch.

Instantly I felt my anger and jealousy again, but this time I stopped myself. After all, what good would it do to get angry? So I did not say a word.

31

I just walked into the other room, and the thought of them being together went into my heart—a clean sword of pain.

Then something curious happened: I felt more myself than I had in days.

As much as I can hardly stand this distance I feel between Susan and me, something is starting to happen when I just allow myself to feel my pain. It is as if I come into the quiet center of a storm. The clouds of anger and jealousy clear, and I actually feel more connected to myself. I feel deeper. I even feel taken care of, as if this situation were not just a disaster, as if it were actually a gift—for me maybe even more than for Susan. At those times I know I can let Susan go if that is what she wants.

The moment I start arguing with Susan, however, I lose this sense of peace. Then I feel the unfairness of Susan being with David. I feel desperate that I might lose her. But in those moments I suppose I am not *innocently* feeling my pain. For when I am fighting Susan, I am actually fighting my pain, and that is when my pain becomes unbearable.

For most of our marriage I have fought my pain. When Susan would confront me on my selfishness, instead of feeling the pain of my selfishness, or even the pain of having hurt her, I would react defensively. I would become incensed: "How dare you call me selfish?" I just wanted her to stop complaining, so things could return to status quo.

I have wasted a lot of pain in my life. But then I had no idea pain could serve a purpose. I had no idea that pain could cause me to feel differently, think differently, act differently, could cause me to change in a way that I always wanted to, but never knew how.

I remember reading somewhere that the purpose of pain is wisdom. I am starting to think this is true, but I see now that we can only find this out after our pain has changed us, after we let ourselves feel it innocently.

I just realized something else about this situation with David and Susan. For years I have had a secret fear in my life: that Susan might someday get involved with another man. Not that I consciously acknowledged this fear. Consciously, I told myself that she would never be foolish enough to jeopardize her relationship with me. I told myself that she was lucky to have me. Yet deep down I knew that if she ever became involved with another man, it would be the one humiliation I could not bear; it would be too painful.

So I bolstered my confidence and told myself that she would never make such a mistake. Instead of looking at my insecurity, I remained self-absorbed, and our relationship suffered. Now that she has the chance for a nurturing relationship with someone else, she may take it.

Interesting how that works: I refused to face my worst fear when it was just a fear, so it became reality.

The Miracle of Vulnerability

Love is not love until love's vulnerable.
>   —Theodore Roethke

Last night, as we were getting ready for bed, Susan asked me how my day had gone. This was a change of pace—we had hardly been saying good night to each other. So we ended up talking for a while. It was as if we were strangers and friends at the same time; there was a good feeling between us, but we could not totally relax and be comfortable either. Then just as we were finishing, Susan said she could not believe how I was changing. She said she really appreciated my vulnerability.

Vulnerability has always been a vague term for me, so before I went to bed I looked it up in the dictionary. *Webster's Ninth New Collegiate Dictionary* defines vulnerable as "1 : capable of being physically wounded   2 : open to attack or damage : ASSAILABLE   3 : liable to increased penalties but entitled to increased bonuses after winning a game in contract bridge."

I am not sure that these definitions fit. Susan must have meant that I seem more open to feelings I previously did not allow myself to feel, especially pain. But this is not the same as simply allowing myself to be hurt. I am not allowing myself to be hurt. I am just trying to be more honest; I am letting myself feel what I have been avoiding all these years, without defensively protecting myself.

If we open our hearts—to the world, to those around us, and to ourselves—then we can be hurt, but then we can also grow.

One essential ingredient of this kind of vulnerability seems to be trust—trust that life is not out to ruin me, that life is on my side (not just my side, but everybody's side). Trust is the antidote for defensiveness. When I trust, I do not have to avoid pain. I do not have to keep life out. I can feel that life is a friend; I can allow life to carve its meaning in me.

In marriage, vulnerability seems essential. For intimacy is a challenge of the heart; whether we grow from that challenge or create misery for each other depends first upon our openness to feel. That is, upon our vulnerability.

A Healing Solitude

The nurse of full-grown souls is solitude.
                                        —James Russell Lowell

I have been home from my trip for just over two weeks. Susan and I are starting to connect more, and her interest in David appears to be fading. She keeps saying how much I am changing.

It's funny, the first couple of times Susan said this, I felt myself jump at the hope that she would forget about David and recommit to me. But instantly I felt myself lose depth. So I am learning not to jump at hoping for anything. I am only focusing on staying in my own integrity.

When I try to put my finger on just what that integrity is, in addition to vulnerability the word "solitude" keeps coming to mind. Not solitude in the sense of simply being alone, but in the sense of settling into myself, being more *with myself* and with a deeper level of personal meaning in my life.

I think Susan is also feeling some of this inner solitude; she is certainly acting more like her own person. Perhaps her relationship with David is opening the door to solitude for her, as much as it is for me.

Rainer Maria Rilke once wrote: "A good marriage is that in which each appoints the other guardian of his solitude." It strikes me that we never guarded each other's solitude before. In fact, just the opposite: we *depended* upon each other for our happiness, and this dependency gradually eroded our sense of individual solitude. I would not even be surprised if much of my selfishness, and Susan's attraction to David, were both reactions to this loss of solitude in our marriage.

So life had to take over and guard our solitude for us, by giving us David.

Marriage is a solitary journey as much as it is a journey of two together. After all, the first step to connect with each other must be to connect with ourselves. Otherwise, what is the meaning of intimacy?

The Art of Dying

*Even as the stone of the fruit must break,
that its heart may stand in the sun, so must
you know pain.*

—Kahlil Gibran

For the past week or so, we have been relating in a friendly, even playful way. I haven't asked Susan about David, but I know that she has not been seeing him as much lately. Then last night Susan made my favorite dinner: lasagna. At one point during dinner, I apologized for all the years of selfishness. She apologized for the pain she had been putting me through. We hugged, and then something happened that has never happened our entire relationship: we both cried.

While we cried, a huge weight lifted off me. Not only were we finally connecting, not only were we feeling our love for each other, but I could feel that I was letting go of something I had held onto for a long time. It was as if all that we had been through over the past month had gradually eaten away at something in me, something that had kept me from giving myself to Susan. As we cried together, whatever that was, finally died.

I have heard the term *ego-dying*. I have even used it myself. But I never knew what it meant until that moment when the wall of non-feeling I had put between Susan and myself crumbled. All my ideas of myself as self-sufficient and self-contained dissolved; my inhibition over showing my emotions dissolved; a part of me truly did die. Yet I never felt more alive.

And I finally understood why ego-dying has received so much press over the centuries in so many cultures: because dying compresses years of growth into a moment of feeling.

Looking back, I see that I could have been dying and growing since the day we first met. Every time I held out in an argument, every time I wanted things my way, every time I wanted Susan to change instead of me—these were all perfect chances to die. Perhaps they would not have been so cataclysmic, but dying just the same. As it was, I had to catch up for the dying I had not done all these years.

Life offers innumerable experiences, but right now it all seems to boil down to this:

1) Catching our opportunities to die.
2) Suffering the results of not dying.
3) Enjoying the fruits of having died.

As we finished dinner, Susan told me that it was over between David and her. She said that they had both sensed the end coming for a couple of weeks. Then yesterday afternoon they had met and agreed that they should not be anything more than friends—really just friends.

So for the first time in almost two months, last night Susan and I made love. It felt like the first time ever.

CHAPTER III

Love's First Challenge

Shadows of Love

They do not love that do not show their love.
—Shakespeare

We have been back together for almost two months now, and for the most part our relationship has been effortlessly gliding in a state of grace. But just lately some minor challenges are coming up for Susan and me.

Like today. Susan asked me to help her clean the kitchen. I had plenty of other things to do, and the moment she asked, I felt irritated. It was a familiar reflex. I hadn't felt it much lately, but I had often felt that irritation in the past when Susan had asked me for help. So for a few moments, I hovered between helping her and telling her that I had too much to do. Then it hit me: What am I thinking? I can't expect to glide on our love. I can't rest on simply feeling my love for Susan. I have to *act* on my love for her.

So I did.

Looking back over our years together, I can see that my love for Susan has been far too passive. How many times have I felt a moment of appreciation or love and let it pass by unnoticed? How many times have I let the chance to act on love slip away? And when I have acted, it has often been on anything but love. Without even thinking about it, I could become irritable, angry, or selfish. But act on my love? Rarely. On holidays and birthdays maybe.

The problem is not just that I have been taking Susan for granted, though that is part of it. For some reason, I have also assumed that feeling my love for Susan should be enough, as if Susan should telepathically tune into my love for her and realize that my feelings are what really count. After all, don't my feelings mean more than mundane actions like helping with the dishes?

But what good is my love if it stays in my heart, hidden from the world and from Susan? Love can be an action as simple as doing the vacuuming, surprising Susan with flowers, making dinner for her, or giving her an unexpected hug. Love can even be as simple as giving Susan more attention than I give to the TV. Yet if I fail to make these simple gestures, if I fail to act on my love, then no matter how much love I feel, my relationship with Susan will not be one of love, but one of neglect.

Love *means* action, because when we fail to act on our love, our love soon fades into familiarity.

Too Busy to Love?

Today I got another lesson on acting on love.

It started this morning at work. I was standing at the copier, when suddenly the thought of Susan at her most beautiful and womanly best filled my heart and mind. For a few moments I basked in my appreciation for her. But did I take a break and make a surprise phone call to say I love you? No. Did I scribble a quick love note or even make a note to do something special for her later? No again. By the time I finally did get home, my momentary appreciation had been buried under a mountain of concerns regarding work. I walked in the door and barely muttered hello.

Even if I am too busy to act on my love in a given moment, I can still make a mental note to do something special for her later. I do not have to let my love slip by unnoticed. Time and space need not bar acts of love any more than they bar feelings of love.

Romance Inside Out

*Whatever joy there is in this world
All comes from desiring others to be happy,
And whatever suffering there is in this world
All comes from desiring myself to be happy.*

—Shantideva

This morning I went on an appointment in the south end of town. Afterward, I decided to stop and eat lunch in nearby Seward Park. It was one of those sunny fall days that are all too rare in Seattle; I was not about to spend it in the office. I parked my car, followed a trail through the woods to the beach, and made myself comfortable on the grass above the shore. In the sun and cool lake breeze, I leisurely ate my sandwich.

Susan had introduced me to this park in our courting days, but we had not been back in years. As I sat there eating, all the sunny afternoons and moonlit nights we had spent there together came back to me, and with them, the whole feeling of our relationship back then. I remembered how, from the day we fell in love, a selfishness that had characterized my life to that point was instantly transformed into caring for her. I wanted to give to her, to make her happy, to protect her. I doubt if I had ever before felt so gracious, so aware of another's needs.

Then, as I sat there in the grass reminiscing, it suddenly struck me that what was most miraculous about those early days together *was how our love had re-created us.* Feeling our love was wonderful, but what a transformation that feeling caused in us! If we had only appreciated this then, who knows where we would be now.

But neither of us appreciated this, and somehow, bit by unseen bit, selfishness began to creep back in. Within the first weeks of marriage, we both began acting to contradict our love, until the romance that spurred us to treat each other to the best of ourselves melted away, and the honeymoon ended.

Yet perhaps this is part of the plan of marriage—a secret conspiracy of life. First we are given a glimpse of love, of what is highest within us, and that glimpse draws us into the commitment of marriage. Only later do we find out that our hearts have caught us in a relationship intimate enough to uncover all that remains unconscious and self-centered within us. Then either our unconsciousness and selfishness assert themselves (in which case we end up unhappily married or divorced), or we finally face the task of making the unconscious conscious, and the self selfless.

The intimacy of marriage offers plenty of promise —of love, of happiness, of fulfilling our dreams, but marriage offers only one guarantee: that things will not go exactly as either of us want or expect. And this is the only way that marriage can become a journey of growth.

Actually, even though I was transformed when we first fell in love, that transformation could not have lasted. For my love back then was based on need: the need for companionship, the need to feel loved, sexual need, to name only a few. Sooner or later, I would have had to find out that Susan could not perfectly fill all my needs (or that even if she could, this would not perfectly fulfill me). The honeymoon was bound to end.

A growing relationship cannot mean perpetuating romantic love. We cannot stay at the level of dependency. Rather, a growing relationship means unfolding our own power to love, to give, to be our highest Self. A growing relationship means turning romantic love inside out—from love that takes, to love that gives. Giving makes love more than just a passing feeling. Giving makes love a state of being.

Fear of Giving

The love we give away is the only love we keep.
—Elbert Hubbard

Getting married is a huge decision for anyone, but I remember that for me this decision brought on a state of panic unlike any I had ever experienced. In the throes of that panic I even cancelled our wedding—twice. If Susan would have put up with it, I would have cancelled a third, maybe even a fourth time.

What made marriage such a frightful prospect for me was my unspoken fear that marriage would not only force me to give of myself, but to give *away* myself. I feared that once married, I would no longer have the freedom to pursue my own happiness.

Although I overcame my panic enough to go through with the wedding, my fear did not end there. It follows me, even to this day. Thanks to this fear, for most of our marriage I have jealously guarded my freedom. What I wanted—my plans, my needs—I made my priorities. I gave to Susan now and then, but underneath it all, my freedom came first.

Now I see that I felt this fear only because I was so inexperienced in giving: whether single or married, my happiness depends upon becoming an expert giver. Giving, not taking, is how we liberate the happiness hidden within our being.

One thing is certain: I am not naturally giving. This may be why, for me, marriage is the perfect path. (If only to defeat selfishness a better situation could not be invented than marriage.) Still, I can only give what I have, and this is another fear related to giving: maybe there is a reason for my selfishness. Maybe I do not have that much to give.

So how can I grow so that I will have more to give? Through giving. Nothing draws me out of unconsciousness, out of a self-centered subjectivity, like giving.

Whenever I feel that I cannot give, why not try taking time out from that feeling—and give something?

A Question of Compatibility?

Something else about giving: it clears the mind, just as selfishness clouds it . . .

In the first few years of our marriage, my lack of giving was a constant point of contention. Susan used to frequently argue that I never did anything to help her. Well, one day, rather than argue the point, I decided I would air some doubts I was having about our marriage.

"You know," I said, interrupting her appeal for help, "I'm starting to wonder if we are meant for each other."

"What are you talking about?" asked Susan.

"I mean it," I said. "You act like you want me to be a different person. If you have to always nag me so much, maybe we are just not right for each other."

Susan gave me a look that would turn a stone to dust and without a word walked into the other room. I followed her and insisted she tell me what she was thinking.

"I never wanted you to be a different person," she said after some prodding. "I just wanted some help. And it's cruel to say you doubt our marriage."

"But I do wonder if we are right for each other," I insisted. "How do you know we didn't make a mistake in getting married?"

"Why don't you face it," she said, "you just don't want to give." Then she left the house in tears.

I did not think so then, but Susan was right: if I had really wanted to figure out whether or not we were meant to be together, all I would have had to do was to start giving and then see how I felt about our marriage. Until I did this, until I rose above the fog my selfishness cast over my judgement, I had no right to speculate on our compatibility.

Whenever I feel doubts, or feel lost, or ready to shuck everything, I should ask myself if there is some way in which I am not meeting my challenge to grow. Am I being selfish? Lazy? Reactive? Insensitive? Next I should try imagining the positive action that would counterpoint my present response, then set my doubts aside for a while and do my best to manifest that positive action.

The more I move with the forces of personal growth in our relationship, the more what once seemed to be gravity turns out to be grace.

My relationship with Susan consistently requires that I grow in a way that single life and no previous relationship ever has. This in itself speaks well of our compatibility.

In Sickness and in Health

A few weeks ago both of us were fighting a losing battle against the flu. To make matters worse, I was up against a tight deadline at work, and Susan also had a grueling schedule (she is a massage therapist). Things really got rough one day, when Susan had four clients scheduled to come to our home for massages. Mid-morning she burst into our bedroom where I was working, declared that she did not even have time to clean up the house for her clients, and asked why couldn't I ever help.

"What are you talking about? I've been helping you a lot lately," I replied.

"I don't see how you can sit there and say that!" she said, and walked out of the room.

My precarious creativity blasted to smithereens, I struggled to remind myself that Susan was not feeling any better than me. I followed her into the kitchen and gave her a hug.

"Feeling overwhelmed?" I asked.

"Yeah," she admitted, "I know you've been helping, but I feel like *I* need the massage."

There was still half an hour before her first client, so I gave her a quick back rub and we cleaned up together. Suddenly we felt our love again.

Giving makes love actual.

Later, as I tried to get back into my writing, a thought kept nagging at me: maybe I had slipped some in my giving to Susan lately. So I made a secret resolution to give at least two things each day to make her life easier.

It has been almost three weeks now, and so far I have stuck to my resolution. Each night at dinner I mentally check to make sure I have given at least two things to help her in someway; if I haven't given two things, then I get them done before bed. Giving two things a day may not seem like much, but it is doing wonders for our relationship. I do not know how many times in the past week Susan has said, with a look of awe on her face, "I can't believe how much you're changing."

A marriage can be improved in many ways, but I cannot think of one that does not have something to do with giving.

Love Not a Feeling?

He who wants to do good knocks at the gate; he who loves finds the gate open.
> —Rabindranath Tagore

Today at work John and I were talking about our marriages. He told me how he and his wife nearly divorced last year over an affair he had, but that with the help of counseling they were now doing very well. I told him what I have been realizing lately: that I need to act on my love more. He enthusiastically agreed with this idea. He even quoted something he had heard, that "love is not a feeling at all, but an intention to nurture each other."

I had also heard this before, and in a way this is just what I have been realizing. Yet when John said this, I could not help feeling that something was missing. At the time I wasn't sure just what it was, but now that I am writing this it seems obvious.

Love *is* more than just a feeling; love means nurturing and giving. Yet to say that love is not a feeling at all is taking a good point too far. After all, what is more fulfilling than to *feel* love deeply and purely? Giving our love to each other is not the only goal of our growth. Feeling our love is every bit as crucial, for if feeling ever leaves our marriage we are in trouble.

Feeling is what makes love a joy, as well as a challenge. If love was not a feeling, then giving love would be a dry experience. Like when I do not feel my love, yet force myself to give. Then no matter how good my intentions may be, my giving lacks richness; I may even feel irritated while giving.

No, intention alone is not enough. The key to giving does not lie in simply forcing myself to give. I need to connect with my feelings, for true nurturing is *based* on feeling. When I feel my love for Susan, and I have an intention to nurture her, and I act on that intention, then I nurture not only Susan but myself.

I have often felt thrilled by the power of our love; rarely, if ever, by the power of my intentions.

Actually, the intention to nurture is already contained within the feeling of love. When I feel my love for Susan, I naturally desire to give to her. When I feel my love for her, the intention to nurture her comes spontaneously. The challenge lies in translating that intention to nurture into action. Love may be spontaneously nurturing, but great effort is needed to remove old habits—laziness, thoughtlessness, selfishness—from the path of love.

Shopping Satori

I find good people good,
And I find bad people good
If I am good enough.

—Lao Tsu

I recently reread Erich Fromm's *The Art of Loving*. One point that Fromm made particularly struck me: "Love of one person implies love of man as such." I take this to mean that if my love for Susan is real, then not only will I love Susan, but my love will extend to others—even to strangers. I will be a loving person.

So I have been asking myself: Do I wish for the happiness of people I do not even know? People I see walking down the street, or in the store, or driving on the freeway? I am discovering that I am not yet a loving person.

For instance, last week I went shopping. I found myself brushing past people without giving them so much as a thought, which is how I have shopped for as long as I can remember. But how can I love someone if I do not even notice them? So I tried to do at least that much: just notice people. I did not try to say hello or even to smile. I just tried to look for their quality as persons.

It was hard. I was already tired from shopping (the moment I step foot in a mall I am ready for a nap), but soon I started to feel more alert, and by the end of the day, I *was* noticing people more; I even felt drawn to them. And for the first time in years, I actually enjoyed shopping.

Attention is the beginning of love.

Today while driving home from work, I discovered an even more advanced exercise for expanding love: overlooking what people do. This comes in especially handy during rush hour.

Becoming a loving person means doing with everyone just what I try to do with Susan, and with Susan just what I should try to do with everyone: notice their humanness, be alert to their needs, and give what I can. Unless I can do at least this much, my love for Susan is little better than a dream.

CHAPTER IV

The Inner Dance

In the Name of Growth

For even as love crowns you so shall he
crucify you. Even as he is for your growth
so is he for your pruning.

Even as he ascends to your height and
caresses your tenderest branches that quiver
in the sun,

So shall he descend to your roots and
shake them in their clinging to the earth.

—Kahlil Gibran

Today when I arrived home from work, Susan asked me to spend time with her and Gemma (our daughter) while she made dinner. I had been trying to write in my journal more, so I told Susan that I would be with them later.

"You never spend time with us anymore," she replied. "You may write about growing, but you're going back to your old impersonal and invulnerable self."

I could hardly believe my ears.

"What! I'm just as vulnerable as ever," I said.

At which point Susan simply shook her head in disgust and left me to my writing.

Now I am wondering if Susan has a point: I have been writing a lot lately and not spending much time with her and Gemma . . .

Resisting growth can come in many forms. Even in the guise of growth.

I am beginning to realize that defining my priorities from where I am now is like insisting I know the best way to the top of a mountain I have never climbed before. If I am to grow, I cannot just focus on what I want. I also need to stay open to discovering what life wants for me.

This is a matter of vulnerability. Vulnerability does not allow me to congratulate myself for a good day at work while telling Susan that I am too tired to give her a hand. Vulnerability does not allow me to revel in my solitude and ignore that I have not played with my daughter in days. When I am vulnerable, each moment impresses me with its meaning, and with its possibilities for growth.

It is important to feel a deep inner relationship with myself. But that inner relationship with myself must also open me to others, or else it is not yet real.

Reply to St. Jerome

Matrimony is always a vice, all that can be done is to excuse it and to sanctify it; therefore it was made a religious sacrament.

—St. Jerome

Something else about last night when Susan asked me to spend time with her and Gemma: I was faced not only with a demand to give time, but to find meaning. I needed to see, and feel, that by giving of myself I would grow. Once I stopped reacting and looked within, I did find this meaning. It did not take half an hour of self-reflection, just a few moments, just long enough for me to feel my resistance and then die to it.

Another way of looking at this: thirty seconds of conflict with Susan showed me where I was in conflict with life. I might have written in my journal for years to find this out.

Marriage is that intimate relationship which tugs and pulls at two egos in order to create the fulfillment of each—if only we can humble ourselves enough to cooperate.

Solitude Inside Out

Last Friday we had dinner with our friends, Carol and Robert. Actually we had dinner with Carol; Robert was delayed by a game of racquetball. We had dessert with Carol and Robert.

After dessert the subject of marriage came up. Robert and Carol shared that after a couple years of marriage they had both reached a point of feeling smothered by their relationship. They had felt as if they were losing their individual freedom and self-identities. Finally, however, they had arrived at a solution: spending more time pursuing entertainment and friendships apart from each other.

Suddenly, what I had seen in Robert and Carol's relationship made sense to me. That was why Robert had so casually walked in late for dinner. That was why I sometimes had the feeling that Robert and Carol were hardly married at all, that they were more like two singles living together.

I respect Robert and Carol's efforts to maintain their individual identities within their relationship, and perhaps the solution they found was necessary for them. Yet I am just beginning to find that if I throw myself wholeheartedly into my marriage, if I fully accept my marriage as my path (with all its challenges), then my relationship with Susan *adds* to my self-identity; I become more myself.

Sometimes I do need to spend time alone or with my own friends. I also need to give Susan time to do the same. But if this becomes the *modus operandi* of our marriage, then we may miss out on much that our relationship offers. Marriage exists not just to preserve our self-identities, but to expand them.

I cannot gain a full self-identity by living half of anything, especially not half a marriage.

Our growth cannot depend upon each other; we should not see each other as the motivation or source of our individual growth. We must each seek the center of ourselves. Yet our relationship is at the heart of this search.

Football Anyone?

This afternoon I met Robert at his athletic club for lunch. Over a heaping salad he told me that he had been taking a course on manhood, and he highly recommended that I enroll as well. I tried not to take it personally.

"What do you mean a course on manhood?" I asked.

"It's a course," he replied (in a noticeably deeper voice than usual), "for men to develop their identity as men."

"Well, what do you study?"

"Mostly we just get together and do things. You know, play golf, go to football games, just relate as men."

Then he suggested that we get together at least once a week without our wives—just us guys.

"Besides," he continued, "Carol and I have been fighting a lot lately, and I just have to get out of the house."

Again I think Robert's impulse is a good one. He needs more space. But perhaps what he really needs is more inner space, more of a sense of inner solitude. For when someone feels a deep sense of inner solitude, he naturally taps a current of manhood (or I imagine in the case of a woman, of womanhood). The challenge, however, is that finding this inner space means opening the door to one's pain. Which is why I cannot help but imagine that the key to Robert's manhood lies not on the golf course or in the football stands, but at home.

Backsliding

The line between failure and success is so fine that we scarcely know when we pass it: so fine that we are often on the line and do not know it.

—Elbert Hubbard

For the past several months, Susan and I have really been connecting. We have both felt our love and giving to each other has been easy. But just in the past week or two, something has changed; we are not paying as much attention to each other. Instead of taking our usual walk together every night, we have been watching TV. Last night I realized how bad things are getting: Susan turned down the TV during a commercial so we could talk, and I rushed to turn it back up because I did not want to miss it.

The amazing thing is how subtly this change has taken place. We have not had any fights, we have not been irritated with each other—just a little laziness slipping in, just a little of the feeling that we could coast for a while, and the depth of feeling and intimacy we felt is suddenly going flat. I have always thought that the difference between a stagnant relationship and a growing relationship was like night and day—a huge difference. But what has been happening to us lately makes me think that the difference may be ever so slight, perhaps the difference of only one or two percent: the almost imperceptible difference between having or not having an edge.

Life (and a relationship) is not stagnant; it is a process. To be fully in life we must also be in process, and life does not stop for a moment.

When we put less emphasis on our relationship, laziness and passivity tend to creep in. Our relationship loses the edge that makes it vital and fulfilling. Then the thought of trying to get our edge back seems like pure drudgery: "Just be together tonight? Oh, but I really wanted to watch the eight o'clock movie. Sure I have seen it before, but it's a great movie. Anyway, I just need to relax."

Still, no one is so alert as to always stay on the edge. Losing our edge now and then is part of growing in a relationship, for growth is not a linear process. When breaking new ground, a little dirt always falls back into the hole.

But this is no excuse to stop digging.

Tonight we kept the TV off and took a walk together. It was not such a chore after all. In fact, it was the most satisfying part of our day.

Tale of Two Towels

Last week I had to fly to Houston for an overnight business trip. Some old friends of ours who live in Houston, Sonia and Tom, invited me to stay with them. I accepted their invitation, Sonia made a delicious spanikopita, and the three of us visited until after midnight.

By the time I got into the shower the next morning, Tom had already left for work. My first appointment was not for a couple hours yet, so I had time to spare. I finished my shower and was about to shave when Sonia knocked on the door.

"Can I come in for a sec? I need to get something."

I wrapped a towel around myself and opened the door. Sonia was also wrapped in a towel. She walked in, said she needed the hair-dryer, but then seemed to want to talk.

"It sure is good to see you again, Henry," she said, looking into my eyes warmly.

"Yeah. It's good to see you guys again too."

Then she took a step toward me, and the next thing I knew she was giving me a long, friendly hug.

I have never been much of a hugger—I usually feel a bit awkward—but all of my past experiences of awkward hugging were nothing compared to this. Sonia was a beautiful woman, a beautiful *married* woman and a friend, naked under this towel. As bath towels go it was even kind of scanty.

My mind began to race: Is this really just a friendly hug? If so, couldn't it have waited until we were wearing something more than towels? Is she really that innocent or what? But Susan once told me that Sonia has had several affairs—scratch the innocence theory.

For a moment I wondered what to do. I knew that the slightest response from me and we would be in bed together. One voice inside my head was saying *Whoa! This could be nice . . .* Another voice was saying *Don't do it! Think of Susan. Think of Tom. You will regret it.*

The second voice won out. I did nothing. I just could not hurt Susan that way, or Tom, or even Sonia. Our hug ended uneventfully, and Sonia exited, hair-dryer in hand.

For the most part, afterward I felt pretty good about my self-restraint. An affair is one secret I would not have wanted to keep from Susan. But I admit that at times over the past few days, I have wondered what it would have been like . . .

When I think of fidelity abstractly, as a moral ideal, then fidelity seems to pose an imposition on my personal freedom. Yes, I can restrain myself, but there is still some part of me wishing that once in a while it would be nice if I did not have to.

Yet this feeling of imposition disappears when I see fidelity from a different perspective. When I think of how much Susan and I have grown together, how much we have given to each other (especially how much Susan and our relationship has given to me), then being true to her becomes something I *want* to do. It becomes a natural part of my love for her.

In the long run, being true to each other cannot simply be a matter of ethics or of religious precept, but must become our whole-hearted desire—an expression of our tenderest feelings for each other.

To put it another way: our marriage becomes what we conceive it to be. If we conceive of our marriage as the gift of growing together, then gradually we realize that this is what it has been all along. Then remaining true to each other becomes a much simpler affair.

Marriage holds us to a form in which life can create our fulfillment. Therein lies its sanctity.

It is gratifying to realize that we have become so close, that being true to Susan is the same thing as being true to myself.

Seeking Perfection

The supreme virtue here is humility, for the humble are they that move about the world with the love of the real in their hearts.

—Wallace Stevens

A few days ago I again talked with John at work about marriage. I told him how growth had gradually become the whole context for our marriage. This time he shook his head in disagreement.

"What are you trying to do, Henry, have the perfect marriage or something?"

His sudden cynicism took me off guard.

"I doubt if a perfect marriage is even achievable," I replied weakly. "All I know is, before trying, we enjoyed being married a lot less."

Later, I wondered from John's question if he thought we were a bit arrogant. Yet yearning for perfection is very different from thinking I *am* perfect. In fact, we only yearn to grow when we realize how imperfect we are.

Besides, we have never tried to have the perfect marriage. Whatever growth we have experienced together has not come by yearning for a better marriage. It has come by being married, while yearning to love, selflessly.

CHAPTER V

A Communion of Feeling

Communication Janus-Style

Love is possible only if two persons communicate with each other from the center of their existence.
> —Erich Fromm

I had set today aside to write. I woke up early and was getting ready to start, when Susan lifted her head from her pillow and asked me what I was doing.

"I'm writing today," I answered.

She propped herself up on her elbows.

"But don't forget, we're going to my parents' house today," she said.

"What? I thought you said next weekend."

"But David and Gayle couldn't make it then. I'm sorry, I forgot to tell you."

"Well, forget it. I'm writing today," I said, then stomped off into my office.

A little while later, however, guilt got to me. I would have to go to her folks, I realized, for I had stayed home the last time they had invited us over. This irritated me. I suddenly felt the need to "communicate."

I walked back into our bedroom and called upon all my knowledge of the art of communication—every tidbit I had ever heard third hand. It all boiled down to *communicate what you feel.* I nudged Susan's shoulder to wake her up. She opened her eyes halfway.

"The way you forget to keep me informed is really bugging me," I said.

"You woke me up for that?"

"Yes. I want to know why you don't care enough about my schedule to tell me what's going on."

At this, she moaned and rolled over.

"You see what I mean? You don't care." So saying, I pulled her covers off.

"Don't!"

"We need to talk."

"About what?" she said, pulling the covers back over her.

"About keeping me informed. About showing a little consideration."

"Consideration! Look what you just did to me. You don't consider *me.* I work hard. I need my rest."

"I need to write."

"So go write, and let me sleep," she said and pulled the covers completely over her head.

So much for our talk.

Now I am sitting here writing, and I cannot shake the feeling that somewhere I went wrong "communicating my feelings."

Perhaps it was a mistake to start off by saying that she made me angry. After all, saying this showed that I had already judged her: *she* made me angry, it was all *her* fault. I was blaming, not communicating. I also could not wait to communicate my anger. It had to be right now. That should have been a sure tip-off that I was reacting.

Communication must mean more than simply communicating feelings. For one thing, it is probably a good idea to look at my feelings before trying to communicate them.

It is easy to erupt with such statements as "I'm angry," or "You're totally irresponsible"; but what does this accomplish? Communicating should bring us closer. It should create a mutual understanding and respect that allows our intimacy to grow. Ultimately, communication should create a communion of feeling between us. This won't happen by blaming and attacking each other.

This morning with Susan, underneath my frustration, I did want her to understand how I felt, so that we could go on with our lives in accord. Yet I blamed her, I unloaded my anger and irritation. No wonder she responded the way she did. Who in their right mind wants to commune with those feelings?

The more we communicate, the more chances we have to feel together. But when we communicate the wrong things (or in the wrong way), we end up feeling the wrong things together.

Also, the greater my urgency to communicate, the more volatile my feelings, and the greater the likelihood that I am resisting the task of inner growth. In other words, the worst time to communicate may be when I feel that "I just *have* to communicate."

For me at least, the biggest challenge of communication is to hold off on communicating until I have first looked within. Until I do that, I can only communicate my reactions. But if I look within, I can work through my reactions. I can find my *deepest* feelings and then communicate those.

This morning I communicated my anger, but anger was not my deepest feeling. I was not angry to my core. Underneath my anger was my disappointment that I rarely have time to write. I wanted Susan to understand this, so that she could help me plan my time by keeping me informed. Before I could communicate this to Susan, however, I had to discover it for myself. That would have meant connecting with my own inner feelings.

Communication means not only communicating with each other, but with ourselves. Only then can communication become what it was meant to be: a communion of feeling.

Communicating from the Core

Go to your bosom;
Knock there, and ask your heart what it doth know.
                                                    —Shakespeare

Last night Susan showed me what it means to really communicate what you feel. I was reading in bed, and Susan was waiting for me to turn off the light. Finally she interrupted my reading.

"I realized today," she said, "that what you have been doing or not doing has not been what's bothering me at all."

I looked up from my sales report. She was referring to how little I had been helping her lately. I had been putting in long days at work on a new sales campaign, and over the past few weeks she had grown to resent my lack of participation at home. She knew what pressure I was under at work. She even admitted that her resentment was not rational. Still, she felt it.

"It's just that since I have to do everything around here," she continued, "plus my work, I don't have time to cook a decent meal. I hardly have time to be with Gemma, or with you. I feel more like a work machine than a human being. I know I'm panicking, but I can't help feeling that this is how my life is going to be forever."

I laid down the sales report. Put this way I suddenly understood what she was feeling. Here were no demands, no anger, no negativity—just Susan whom I loved, feeling frustrated, helpless, and vulnerable. So we talked about the pressure I was experiencing at work. I assured her that it was not going to last much longer, and I promised to try to take some of the load off her in the meantime.

Thanks to Susan's vulnerability, not only could I suddenly relate more to her feelings, but so could she: Susan had not liked her resentment any more than I had. Her vulnerability got through to both of us.

True communication does mean communicating how we feel, but how we *really* feel. This happens only when we manage to touch our deepest feelings, feelings that underlie obvious feelings, feelings that require searching just to find them. There, in the core of our feelings, we are most ourselves—most vulnerable, human, and attractive.

Communicating grievances is one thing, but when we communicate with vulnerability how we feel, we remind each other that we are human beings. This draws us closer.

Innocence and Communication

Whoever would become as a child must overcome his youth too.

—Nietzsche

Yesterday Susan said she wanted to hire a house-keeper. I told her that we could not afford one. We argued about it and never came to an understanding.

So while driving home from work this after-noon, I tried to find the best way to tell Susan what I was feeling: We just can't afford a housekeeper. I realize you have too much to do, and I realize I haven't been helping as much as I should, so I promise to help out more.

By the time I reached home, I felt cool, calm, and ready to settle things. I found Susan in Gemma's bathroom, cleaning the tub.

"How was your day?" I asked.

"Busy."

"You know, about this housekeeper thing," I began delicately, "I know you have a lot to do, but we just can't afford a luxury like that."

"It's not a luxury. I need the help."

"Of course it's a luxury. Does everyone have a housekeeper?"

"But other husbands help their wives if the wife is also working," she said, without even a pause in her scrubbing.

"OK, so I'll help you with the cleaning. I was going to say that anyway. But a housekeeper is about the biggest waste of money I can think of. It's ridiculous!"

Funny, driving home from work I had genuinely searched to find my deepest feelings. But then, in that crucial moment of truth when I opened my mouth to tell Susan what I was feeling, I threw in just a little bit of emphasis—to make sure I got my point across. And we did not exactly experience a communion of feeling either . . .

I notice that Susan responds not only to what I say, but also to the way I say it. And this is why my mode of expression needs to be as innocent as my deepest feelings themselves. If communication is to become a communion of feeling, I need to talk not only about my feelings but *from* my feelings. After all, how can I expect Susan to commune with my feelings if I cannot?

Actually, it occurs to me that the first step of innocent communication has nothing to do with talking. Action is the first step, action that gives, delights, and charms the other into a communion of feeling. If I had been giving to Susan by helping her, then our conversation over the bathtub might have turned out very differently (if it would have happened at all). I can ask for loving communication with innocence, only if I have first given my love through action.

Words gain infinitely more power to unite when they rest upon a foundation of giving.

Brevity

A flood of words is never without its fault.
—Proverbs 10:19

Here is another habit that obstructs innocent communication: when Susan and I disagree about something, I tend to come up with not just one reason why I am right, but several, often complete with illustrations, analogies, and/or parables.

But remaking my point in several different ways shows a lack of trust. Either I do not trust in what I am feeling, or I do not trust that Susan will accept what I am feeling. When I hammer my point home, I am trying to make up for my lack of trust by controlling Susan.

This hardly makes for a communion of feeling.

Finding the trust needed to speak from my feelings, simply and with integrity, is not easy. I can sense the tightness in me that wants to control the situation. Even so, I am gradually learning to let go, and when I do, I notice that my feelings become more natural. Then I *can* trust in them more, and so can Susan.

"Be Here Now"

This morning I wanted to make love, but Susan did not want to. She was unusually touchy about it and said that all I wanted was sex, without regard for her. Her comment seemed unfair. I felt hurt by it. I had not exactly thrown myself at her, I had just shown a little affection.

Once Susan was fully awake, she apologized. I told her that it was okay, yet I noticed a thought lurking in the back of my mind: She had hurt me. Did she know that?

No good ever came of such a thought.

Once we have resolved an issue, better to forget about who was right and who was wrong. We also need to keep trusting in each other, even if we make the same mistake a hundred times. Each time the past is the past. We cannot hold onto history; we need to give each other the space to change, by forgiving.

Letting the past dissolve into a new present is at the heart of communication, if communication is to have anything to do with growth.

Techniques for Communicating

This morning I saw a talk show in which the guests were a nationally famous psychiatrist/author and his wife, a psychologist. They had just written a book related to marriage in which communication was a major theme.

Halfway through the show, the talk show host asked her guests to give a demonstration of communication. The wife turned to her husband and expressed how she was hesitant to communicate with him on many issues, because she was afraid that he would become angry. As she spoke, her husband listened attentively, but with a notably professional air. He nodded and grunted every half-sentence like clockwork.

Sensing the mechanical listening of the husband, the talk show host turned to him and asked, "What is this grunting all about? Sounds like maybe some gas pains are involved here."

I felt for the speechless psychiatrist, but the talk show host had a point. This was one expert who appeared to be a victim of his own expertise.

Techniques for communication can be great teaching tools, but if we place too much emphasis on them (or become too good at them), we risk that our communication will lose its innocence and so its essence: feeling.

Communication as a communion of feeling results not from technique, but from a quality of being—of openness, vulnerability, caring, respect —of love.

True, sometimes techniques can help stimulate this quality of being, and when they do, they become tools of genuine growth. The trouble begins when techniques merely *simulate* this quality of being, which usually happens just about the time one becomes a technique enthusiast.

Transcending Words

The words the happy say
Are paltry melody
But those the silent feel
Are beautiful—

—Emily Dickinson

Last night we discovered something else about communication: the best communication happens when we are not talking.

Ultimately, the goal of communication is to transcend words, to dwell together in a luxuriance of feeling. When we simply feel together, look into each other's eyes, be together—this is the highest communication.

The goal of communication lies in the silence between our words.

CHAPTER VI

The Other Face of Love

Creative Conflict

I have come to bring fire on the earth. . . . Do you suppose that I have come to give peace on earth? I tell you, Nay; but rather division.

—Luke 12:49, 51

One does not become enlightened by imagining figures of light, but by making the darkness conscious.

—C. G. Jung

Somewhere along the line, I got the idea that marital conflict was an unfortunate situation that should be resolved in the smoothest way possible. As a result, I assumed that whenever Susan and I were in conflict, we must somehow be off track.

Yet just this morning we had an argument over how I tend to judge people without giving them the benefit of any doubt. I had vaguely known that I do this, but I always assumed that I was perfectly correct in my judgement—so what's the problem?

This time, however, I came away from our argument seeing a smallness in myself I had never seen before. It reminded me of the first time I ever saw myself on videotape; I could hardly believe how awkward I looked, or how nasal I sounded. Only now I suddenly saw a contracted hardness in myself. The experience was humbling to say the least.

Conflict has a way of flaring just where Susan or I are most blind to ourselves (in my case, where I am most selfish, reactive, or critical). As such, those flare-ups shed light on where and how we need to grow. When conflict with Susan can show me where I am in conflict with myself, then how can that be just an unfortunate situation?

Another example of how conflict was necessary for my growth was when Susan and David were together. Until the pain of Susan being with David forced me to change, I remained the "I" that refused to see itself. I had to be pushed to my knees before I would grow.

Still, conflict is risky business. Susan and I might have ended up divorced over David.

Conflict always holds the choice between creative and destructive responses. The choice we make determines the outcome. We can react to conflict with anger, defensiveness, and blame; or respond with forgiveness, openness, and vulnerability. We can end up alienated and bitter, or find our relationship deepening and maturing. Conflict occurs on the cutting edge of our growth, both individually and as a couple. Yet if we refuse to see our need to grow, then that cutting edge can draw our own blood.

The moment one or both of us assumes that "mine is the right way," "I have good reason to defend my position," or "my anger is fully justified," then we are turning the cutting edge of our growth against ourselves and our relationship. We are losing our vulnerability. We are presuming to exist in the perfect relationship to life, to ourselves, to each other, just when this is least the case.

We can respond to conflict with vulnerability and self-honesty, or react with anger and defensiveness. The latter makes us miserable. When we have managed the former, we have not only felt humbled, but also deeply grateful for our marriage.

Because they are so personal, conflicts in marriage hold tremendous power: power to frustrate, to hurt, to anger. The conflicts of marriage penetrate to the heart—right to where they must to deepen us.

What if we could remain vulnerable enough to accept our challenges to grow? Then we wouldn't need to shove each other into growing. Then conflict would become obsolete.

Yes. But until we paid our dues shoving and being shoved, we never knew what vulnerability was.

Marriage is the intimate drama of two growing personalities, and like all good drama, it involves conflict.

Compromising Growth

The course of true love never did run smooth.
—Shakespeare

The past few months I have gotten into a routine of working nearly every Saturday and meditating and writing for a few hours each Sunday. Finally, yesterday Susan objected that I was not spending enough time with the family. After some discussion I gave in. In exchange for having all day Saturday to myself, I agreed to set Saturday night aside to do whatever Susan wanted and promised to make every Sunday a family day. We made a deal.

But now I wonder if we handled this the best way. Not that I regret our compromise; it was fair enough. Yet there is a difference between making deals and growing. Making a deal assumes that the problem exists outside of myself. In this case, in not having enough time to fit everything in. When I assume a problem exists outside of myself, I do not have to *feel* anything to change; I can simply agree, grudgingly or willingly, to adapt to the demands of the situation. But when I allow our problems to register in my feelings, when I allow our problems into my heart, then I not only make a deal, I grow.

The difference is vulnerability.

By simply making deals, we become accustomed to giving a little, and in return, receiving a little—that is, to depriving ourselves of the abundance of our relationship.

By relying on compromise we may also fail to get at the heart of our need to grow. We may grow, but at the rate of old firs, and like firs, remain wooden and stiff in our ways.

Instead of making deals, why not use our differences to look within ourselves, to discover how we can grow? Finding a fair compromise in the midst of argument is not easy. Yet if one or both of us become vulnerable, then compromise will follow effortlessly, even with a sense of grace.

Compromise should follow from, never preempt, growth.

All's Fair in Love?

For years Susan has offered to give me a massage whenever I have wanted one. Because I do plenty of stretching exercises, however, I have rarely felt the need to accept her offer. Then just a few weeks ago, Susan had been having some stiffness in her back. She asked if she could show me some massage moves so that I could give her a good back rub once in a while. I happily agreed. Little did I know that she would need a back rub every few days . . .

Finally last night it came to a head.

"Could you give me a quick back rub?" she asked innocently as we got into bed.

By this point I had given her half a dozen back rubs and had not received a massage from her in months.

"I'm feeling pretty tired," I replied.

"Could you just rub right here?" she pleaded, pointing to the chronically sore spot on her back. "It's killing me tonight."

"OK," I said. But as I reached for the bottle of massage oil on our bed table, I added, "Do you think you could give me a foot massage afterwards?"

I knew it was a mistake as soon as I said it. For a moment Susan did not respond. Then she sat up, her face flushed.

"You mean you won't give me a back rub unless I give you a foot massage?" she asked bitingly.

"Well, you haven't given me a massage in months," I replied. I felt pathetic, but I couldn't help myself.

"Fine," she said. "I'll give you a foot massage. Here, let me do you first."

So she did. In fact, she gave me a very thorough foot massage, and I felt miserable the whole time.

It may be the birthright of every human being to be treated fairly. Yet few issues have caused more tension in our marriage than one or both of us defending this birthright.

In any close relationship, a preoccupation with fairness can become irresistible, but this seems especially true of marriage. After all, of any relationship, shouldn't marriage be an *equal* sharing? (As if Susan washing her half of the dishes will bring me happiness.)

Yet marriage is no excuse for not giving, and so long as we are obsessed with equality in our relationship, we are not giving. For fairness means we give only in relation to what we receive; this is not true giving, but an exchange. Exchanges belong in the marketplace, not in our marriage.

A preoccupation with fairness rests on the illusion that I have not been given enough to give freely to others. This illusion dissolves when I remind myself how much I have been given. Giving is a chance to return just a fraction of all that I have been given. In this sense, giving is an expression of vulnerability, the need for fairness, of invulnerability.

So when I give and Susan doesn't, instead of resenting this, why not see it as another chance to give? I cannot guarantee that Susan will reciprocate, but if I could, I wouldn't be giving.

✳

I wonder if true fairness is even achievable. Massaging each other equally is the least of it. What about cooking half the meals, mowing half the lawn, cleaning half the toilets? Then there is our income. We should each contribute half, naturally. Each giving in a myriad of ways, just as much and no more than the other; it is only fair.

No, I doubt that we could ever achieve such a perfectly fair relationship. And just as well, for that would not be a growing relationship.

A Game of Leapfrog

Here is another, subtler, issue of fairness that has come up between us: Shouldn't a husband and a wife be equally dedicated to growth? Ideally, shouldn't a husband and a wife grow together? Even at the same pace?

Yes. But if our marriage is any indication, two people rarely grow at the same pace, no matter how dedicated to growth they may be. Even if from a distance it appears that a couple is growing in synchrony, I bet that a closer look reveals it is not so. In an intimate relationship, one person often *must* step out ahead—to free the relationship from old patterns, so that both can grow.

Growing in a marriage is often like a game of leapfrog: one leaps while the other stands still. If we insist upon fairness, upon growing simultaneously, we will only wait for each other to take the first leap. Then neither of us moves.

Two people may not be able to grow simultaneously, but they can stagnate simultaneously.

So who should take the first leap? It doesn't matter. When one takes a leap, it opens the possibility (even creates a responsibility) for the other to take a leap. We have to focus only on our own need to grow. Fairness is not the key to leapfrog growing, trust is.

An Advisor in Love

The past few weeks have not been so smooth. We seem to be constantly irritated by each other for one thing or another, and no matter how hard I try to give to Susan, either I cannot give or I resent it when I do.

Then last Saturday we were supposed to go east of the mountains to the wedding of one of Susan's distant relatives. An hour before we were to leave, I told Susan that I had decided to stay home and get some work done around the house. We argued about it for a while, but I stood firm. I had no desire to go, and given the atmosphere between us, the prospect of having some time to myself was irresistible. Susan left for the wedding alone.

Shortly after she left, a stray thought began needling me: What if she gets in an accident? A ridiculous worry, I told myself. A one in a million chance. I pushed the thought aside. Yet this irrational thought persisted so much over the next few hours that I began to feel genuinely concerned. What if I was having some kind of premonition?

By late afternoon my imagination was running wild. I was certain that at any moment I would receive a phone call from a hospital telling me that she had been in an accident. I saw myself driving at breakneck speed to her side. I felt just what it would be like if she were seriously injured—or worse.

Finally, about nine-thirty in the evening I heard our car drive up. A moment later Susan walked in the door, alive and well as ever. Instantly my anxiety dissolved. One thing did not dissolve, however: feeling just how much Susan means to me.

Maybe my premonition was not so false. At least it reawakened me to the preciousness of our relationship.

When things get rough between us, and I would like nothing more than to be alone, then maybe I should try imagining, as vividly as I can, that I *am* alone. Then act on my love. Knowing that someday we will not have each other makes a powerful advisor in love.

Crisis/Opportunity I

We learn geology the morning after the earthquake.
                              —Ralph Waldo Emerson

Several weeks ago I got a call from Jean, the wife
of a close friend; she was in tears. Her husband,
Bill, was threatening to leave her, and she asked if
I would come over and talk with him. I gladly said
I would and left for their house immediately.

Jean and Bill had always had a "let's not get
heavy, life's here to enjoy" approach to their relationship. They had even kidded Susan and me
that our preoccupation with growth was weird.
Still, they had their challenges. Jean was a demanding woman, frequently critical of Bill.
Although Bill appeared to take her demands and
criticism in stride, calmly enduring everything, he
nevertheless seemed aloof and withdrawn in their
relationship.

When I reached their house, I found Jean sitting on the front porch in a state of shock, anger,
and inexpressible pain. I sat down next to her, and
amid sobbing she filled me in on what had happened. Apparently, Bill's pent-up resentment had
finally exploded. He had not only insisted that he
was going to leave her, but that he had never loved
her, and further, that she was beneath him. I did

my best to console her, then we went into the house to talk with Bill.

By this time Bill had calmed down. I asked him to describe, from his perspective, what had been happening between them. For the first time in all the years I had known Bill, he talked about his feelings openly and honestly. Without any sense of condemnation, he calmly described a number of things Jean had done or said, and how they made him feel.

Although at first Jean reacted defensively to what Bill said, little by little she seemed to take much of it in. Then came a significant turning point. Bill acknowledged that many of their problems were his fault for holding everything inside. He also admitted that he had always had great difficulty in being open with his feelings. At this, Jean dropped her defenses. She became genuinely caring about Bill and more vulnerable than I had ever seen her.

As the evening came to a close, they both expressed feeling that their marriage could not have lasted much longer without some change. They knew they had a lot of things to work through, and they intended to see a counselor, but at least they now felt hopeful over the possibilities. Jean even mentioned something she had heard, that in the Chinese language the word *crisis* implies both danger *and* opportunity.

That was three weeks ago. Today I called Jean to see how things were going.

"Oh, we're doing pretty well," she said. "You know, pretty much back to normal. And I'm glad for that. I really couldn't have handled much more of that vulnerability."

I did my best to congratulate her, but I could not help feeling more than a little disappointed.

I know that both Bill and Jean are learning a great deal from what they are going through. I know that I cannot ask them to grow the way I want them to. Yet I also know what vulnerability can do for a relationship.

What is a crisis but the consequence of failing to see hundreds of smaller crisis/opportunities that have existed all along? In which case, the answer to a crisis cannot lie in resolving the crisis once and for all. Rather, it lies in realizing this: each day deserves the vulnerability of a crisis/opportunity.

Crisis/Opportunity II

Today Jean called me, in tears again. It seems that "back to normal" is not agreeing with Bill. She told me that Bill is showing nothing but contempt for her and is again insisting that he wants to leave her.

I know their situation is complex; Bill is being challenged to grow every bit as much as Jean, maybe more. Yet I cannot help feeling that this might be a time for leapfrog growing. For if Jean could sustain the vulnerability she felt the night I was at their house, that might help Bill sort through his feelings (maybe even find his love for her again). Even if it didn't, one thing is certain: at least *she* would be transformed.

They say familiarity breeds contempt. In our experience, however, that is only half the truth. Not familiarity alone, but familiarity with each other's invulnerability breeds contempt.

The Wisest Feeling

We hand folks over to God's mercy, and show none ourselves.

—George Eliot

Last night Susan was out giving a massage to a couple in their home; Gemma and I stayed home watching TV together. While switching channels we happened upon a fund-raising telethon for children in Africa. Deeply moved by the footage of starving and diseased children, we called in our pledge.

After a while I put Gemma to bed and continued watching TV. Susan had said that she would be home by ten, so I thought I would wait up for her. It was nearly midnight, however, before she finally walked in the door; she had been in a car accident. The streets were icy, someone had stopped in front of her, and she rear-ended them. Fortunately, it was just a fender bender.

Once I realized that Susan was fine, I made a few well-placed remarks on her driving. After all, obviously she had been tailgating . . .

Looking back on it today, I cannot believe I said that to Susan. Compassion flows readily at the sight of helpless children, emaciated with hunger or stricken with disease. Much harder, it seems, to feel compassion for one's own spouse.

I might not have seen Susan's pain, but it was there, in the depths of her being. To feel compassion for her, I would have had to have been closer to the depths of my being.

Compassion is wisdom in the form of feeling.

The Way of Wholeness

To come to the pleasure you have not
you must go by a way in which you enjoy not
To come to the knowledge you have not
you must go by a way in which you know not
To come to the possession you have not
you must go by a way in which you possess not
To come to be what you are not
you must go by a way in which you are not
                                    —St. John of the Cross

So many times in the past, the differences between how Susan and I see and do things have been the cause of conflict. But today I was thinking about how different we are from each other, and that I am glad for it.

I tend to be mental, intellectual; Susan tends to be intuitive, feeling. I doubt and question; she trusts and accepts. I am self-disciplined and goal-oriented; she lives in the here and now. I prize my freedom; she cherishes our intimacy. These and other differences permeate nearly every aspect of our lives, from our sex life, to how we save and spend money, to what we will allow ourselves to eat.

We have been attracted to each other by our differences, and our differences have caused innumerable disagreements. Sometimes Susan's qualities have guided our growth, and at other times mine have led the way. But gradually, ever so gradually, we are absorbing what is best in each other and are becoming more whole.

Marriage is a way of growth because it unites us with what we are not.

CHAPTER VII

Anger: The Philosopher's Stone

Happy Birthday?

To be wroth with one we love
Doth work like madness in the brain.

—Samuel Coleridge

A couple of weeks ago, as Susan was headed out the door to go to the store, I reminded her to get a birthday card for my sister.

"I won't have time today," she replied. "I'm just picking up a few things I really need; then I have to be back here in an hour for a massage appointment."

"It will only take you five minutes," I pleaded. "If you don't get it today, I know that we'll both forget."

"I'm already late. I'll get it on Wednesday when I go shopping."

I knew I could not push it any further, so I resolved to "trust." Sometimes, though, trusting is not enough. Both of us forgot about the card until almost a week after my sister's birthday.

When I realized what had happened, I could not resist needling Susan with a light-hearted I told you so. I forgot, however, that Susan has a theory regarding light-hearted I told you so's: they do not exist. As far as she is concerned, I told you so's of any kind are inexcusable gibes. Before I knew it, we were arguing.

After five minutes I declared our argument ridiculous and left the room. Then half an hour later Susan came into my office and started in on it again. As it turned out, that little birthday card led to the worst fight we'd had in two years. Neither of us gave in, and it took until this morning for our lingering irritation to finally dissolve.

Conflict might show us much about ourselves and how we need to grow. Perhaps it can even result in bringing us closer—if, that is, one or both of us rises above our anger. If we are to learn anything from an argument, at some point one of us has to become vulnerable. Only then does conflict become constructive.

So why can't we just get to the constructive part, vulnerability, right from the beginning?

The next time we fight, instead of trying to be right, perhaps we should take on a bigger challenge: see who can get vulnerable first.

Fruits of Resentment

A fit of rage or a sulk has its secret attractions. Were that not so, most people would long since have acquired a little wisdom.

—C. G. Jung

In the early years of our marriage, there were times when I felt I had to show anger to get Susan's attention, as if showing how upset I was would make her change. Like a child with a knife, I wielded my anger in hopes of cutting through what I saw as her invulnerability.

Inevitably, though, Susan took my anger as an invitation to react with anger of her own. Usually, by the time we resolved things, we had both inflicted emotional injuries, and our fighting left distance and distrust between us.

I should have known better; a child with a knife can be dangerous.

Compared to the work of growing, anger appears to offer easy rewards. Anger offers the hope that I can solve our problems by demanding that Susan change. Anger assures me that I am right and Susan is wrong. With anger, I do not have to face my own fault; I also run less risk of being hurt by Susan. Anger can be comforting, if I am comfortable with not growing.

When I am angry, instead of blaming Susan, why not try to see my anger as a chance to learn something about myself? The demand for change is usually much more creative when turned one hundred and eighty degrees—inward. For the source of my anger is never simply outside of myself. It is within me.

Beneficent Blindness

As selfishness and complaint pervert and cloud the mind, so love with its joy clears and sharpens the vision.
—Helen Keller

They say that love is blind, but a far more serious handicap is the lack of love. How many times have I criticized Susan out of anger, only to discover I had misjudged her, or at least did not give her credit where due? This has happened more often than I can say. But how often do I give Susan too much credit out of my love for her? I cannot remember the last time this happened.

When I feel critical of Susan, or of anyone for that matter, I might ask myself: Do I really see their point of view? Do I really know them? For I do not know a person until I fully appreciate them, until I love them. Only through love can I perceive the true condition of another.

In theory, at least, to know someone fully I would have to know them as God knows them. And God, it is said, is Love.

Even practically speaking, love is preferable to criticism. Love nurtures and softens, it creates trust, it paves the way for helping each other to grow. Criticism, however, sparks defenses into action. It polarizes. It undermines trust. It is never selfless. Behind every personal criticism lies a negative reaction, an ego in some degree invulnerable and out of balance; this makes criticism hard to accept, even when it is accurate.

No, when I am trying to help Susan, if there is any one thing as important as feeling my love for her, it is Susan feeling my love for her. Then she can trust me to help her. Then I can trust myself to help her. Even if at times we must confront each other, still we can do so with love. We can support and nurture instead of criticize.

Criticism speaks to the fault within the person; love speaks to the person behind the fault.

If love were blind, there could be no helping each other through love. The more we loved, the more deluded, helpless, and victimized we would become—and the more blinded we would become to each other's need to grow.

But that is not the case. The more we love each other, not only the more clearly do we see each other's beauty, but the more clearly we see that which hides each other's beauty. And if in seeing this, our love does not disappear, if it perseveres, then our love is already drawing forth what is highest in ourselves.

Waiting for Apology

To be angry is to revenge the fault of others upon ourselves.
—Alexander Pope

Just this morning we had an argument. I knew I had a good point, and I believe even now that Susan was being irrational. Yet I also felt my own negative reaction to her irrationality, so I apologized, fully expecting her to do the same. She never did.

Now I am sitting here writing this and feeling just a bit irritated. *Why wouldn't she apologize?* Yet I also realize that her failure to apologize shouldn't matter. Why should that disturb my peace of mind? No, somewhere I am still reacting.

We are the authors of our own misery.

Growing through our relationship means taking responsibility for ourselves. My growth cannot depend upon Susan taking the same step, at the same time, as I. We are bound to be a little out of step with each other; that shouldn't keep us from growing. In fact, our differences in themselves create perfectly designed opportunities for growth. And I have one of those opportunities right now ...

Gorilla Lovefare

Whatever wholesome deeds,
Such as venerating the Buddhas, and generosity,
That have been amassed over a thousand aeons
Will all be destroyed in one moment of anger.
                                        —Shantideva

A few months ago, Susan mentioned to me that one of her friends, Sandra, constantly criticized her husband. Apparently, Sandra is so good at it that she manages to stay calm, while her husband explodes in a defensive rage.

Then today Sandra came over to have lunch with Susan. I walked into the room just as Sandra was explaining that her husband's many faults did not really bother her so much; she just wanted him to grow. "I care about him," she said. "That's why I have to tell him what I see."

"You know," Susan replied, "criticizing Henry never seems to work for me. I've tried, believe me. I've found I just have to focus on my own challenges; then Henry usually follows suit."

At this, Sandra's face turned crimson.

"But why should I have to tip-toe around for Tom?" she said quickly. "I'm always the one trying to grow."

I ate on the patio.

124

A calm voice or a tone of objectivity does not guarantee the absence of anger. In fact, we may only complicate the situation by putting a lie between us and our true feelings. We need to *feel* our anger before we can grow beyond it.

I do sympathize with Sandra, though. Feeling anger is not always as simple as it sounds, for anger comes in many guises. For instance, whenever I find myself thinking, "I just have to let Susan know how I feel," or, "I'm always the one to grow, she needs to grow, too," then I am angry. Or if I want to confront Susan with a fault of hers, then no matter how much I think it is because I care about her, somewhere I'm angry. In fact, anytime I focus on Susan's problem and am not simultaneously humbled by my own, I can rest assured that something has come between my vulnerability and me. That something may not be anger, but if provoked, you can bet it will turn into anger.

Once I feel my anger, then the real work begins. I may have to privately struggle to find forgiveness. I may have to search for the kernel of truth underneath my anger, then communicate that truth with vulnerability—in a way that draws us closer.

In other words, anger is an opportunity. If I fail to take that opportunity, if I simply feel justified in holding onto my anger, then I miss the whole point. My anger exists to stimulate growth, not so much Susan's as my own.

Feelings, even negative feelings, hold tremendous possibilities, if only we can stay in touch with their true meaning. For instance, a little hidden anger can disturb a relationship for a lifetime, but if uncovered and worked through, the same anger can stimulate growth that will deepen our love.

The Greatest Loss

Let not the sun go down upon your wrath.
—Ephesians 4:26

Lunch with Sandra made me remember when we were going through our rough years. We also allowed our anger to build.

It would usually start with one of us offending the other in some way. The one offended would feel justified in anger and would not let it quit. As a result, we would have more and more arguments, until both of us felt mistreated. Finally, getting nowhere with our arguments, the anger would go underground, where it crystallized into something less obvious, but far more deadly than anger: a loss of respect.

Why is a loss of respect so deadly to a relationship? Because like anger it implicitly negates all that is positive and magnifies all that is negative, only it lasts much longer. When angry we focus on each other's faults, but only for a few minutes, maybe for an hour at most until our anger dies down. Losing respect for each other, however, requires subconsciously focusing on each other's faults for days, even for months or for years. A loss of respect is anger hardened into a solid image of negativity.

This must be the pattern of many disintegrating relationships. Anger is allowed to build and gradually undercut a couple's appreciation of each other. As their anger negates what is highest in each other, they unwittingly nurture the worst in each other—and in themselves.

A growing relationship does just the opposite. A growing relationship means growing in our appreciation of each other. Then, as we see more and more clearly what is highest in each other, we draw *that* out in each other—and in ourselves.

Anger rests on blame, and blame on either fear or pain. I notice that when I find the courage to face my fear or to accept my pain, my anger dies a natural death—long before it can turn into a loss of respect.

Digging for Gold

Growing through anger usually means seeing something that I did not see in becoming angry. Here are a few realizations I have had in this process:

Like me, Susan is trying to become happier the best way she knows. Yet we both make mistakes: we stumble and hurt each other and ourselves, we are victimized by our own lack of fulfillment in seeking fulfillment. Short of sainthood, we are all prisoners of this human condition. Why, then, be angry with Susan, when I should be feeling compassion for her?

If Susan has done something unfair or has hurt me, then very likely I am reaping what I have sown in the past. So much has passed between us, so many reactions back and forth, that we are long past saying who is at fault and who is not. Now I can either react and perpetuate our problems, or I can forgive and change the destiny of our relationship.

What am I resenting? That Susan has been unfair, insensitive, negative? If everyone around me treated me with perfect love, how would I

129

grow? For example, how would I overcome my self-importance, which happens to be reacting with pride and anger right now?

Freeing myself from even one of my problems can seem an impossible task. How many problems of my own have I yet to work through? How, then, can I blame Susan for being caught in the grips of her problem, when I have to go through all this just to find forgiveness?

What, exactly, am I feeling? That I am right? That I have every right to defend my position? That my anger is fully justified? But these thoughts cause our relationship to lose grace, even if I am "right." Do I want a rich and fulfilling marriage, or do I want to be right?

Still, even when I take the time for reflection, finding vulnerability in the midst of anger is not easy. Like mining for gold, there is no sure-fire system for becoming vulnerable. Yet I notice that when I make a sincere effort to work through my anger, even if I do not entirely succeed, something in me begins to change. And if my anger finally does give way, and I hit a vein of self-knowledge or of innocent feeling, it often happens when I least expect—at the point I feel most in the dark.

"For it is when I am weak that I am strong" (2 Corinthians 12:10).

Striking It Rich

That man . . . for whom pleasure and pain are the same, he is fit for immortality.

—Bhagavad-Gita, II:15

Perhaps the most popular technique for dealing with anger nowadays is to "accept your anger." Trouble is, I've never understood exactly what this means.

Actually, I do understand accepting my anger in the sense of not condemning myself for being angry. Anger is a normal human emotion—no need to feel down on myself because of it. In fact, I can grow by working through my anger, so in this sense it holds positive possibilities. Yet some people I have talked to seem to have found a deeper meaning in it than this. For them, the phrase "accept your anger" appears to unlock abundant benefits of being angry (and staying that way).

So what does accepting my anger mean? Does it mean that anger is just as good as any other response—patience, understanding, forgiveness? Personally, I would rather be forgiving than angry.

And what about those times when I have not stopped at accepting my anger, but have worked through my anger until I found some vulnerability, some self-knowledge even? Then I did grow through my anger. I doubt that I would have gone to the trouble had I simply accepted my anger.

Perhaps accepting my anger means that if I have good reason to be angry, then I can simply accept my anger. But how do I know when I have good reason? When angry, I usually feel that I have good reason, or I would not be angry. And far too often I have not only avoided growing, but misjudged someone because I felt I had good reason to be angry.

In a word, the concept has always puzzled me. Until this morning. I think that I finally discovered what accepting my anger means . . .

I was sitting in meditation when Gemma burst into the room to ask a question that could have easily waited until later. She knows better, but I answered her question and told her that I would be coming out soon. Five minutes later she burst in with another question. Again I answered her, but more briefly. Finally, she entered with a third question. This time, with eyes still closed, I told her that I would talk to her later. As she left the room, my mind, stilled only a few moments before, now whirled with irritation.

Fully aware of how petty my irritation was, I attempted to recover my shattered composure. Then I had an unexpected realization: My irritation with

Gemma is irrational and petty. No need to take it seriously. It is just some purification, some release of stress; don't resist it.

Suddenly, with no effort on my part, not only did I feel entirely accepting of my anger, but I knew that my anger represented something positive. Not positive at the level at which I was identified with my anger; it was indeed a petty and irrational reaction. Yet it was positive in a larger sense. For as a person on this earth, hopefully growing toward some indefinable state of wholeness, I had to work through my anger. I had to feel it, release it. Doing so was a positive part of my growth.

The instant I felt this, my irritation disappeared.

Yet there was more. A moment later I realized that every negative feeling could also be seen in this light—not only anger, but fear, doubt, depression, anxiety—they all could be accepted. They all were but waves on the surface of the stream of growth.

I also saw that as long as I did not feel this detached acceptance, I slowed my growth to a crawl. Acting on my anger, thinking my anger justified, even reacting against my anger by condemning myself, amounted to blocking my anger from simply passing through me. But standing back from my anger, viewing it as a sign of growth taking place—this allowed it to pass without friction.

Then I had another realization: Positive feelings also qualify for this attitude of acceptance. After all, attachment to happiness, pleasure, success, or security, when thwarted, results in negative emotions: reactions of sadness, pain, self-doubt, anxiety, fear, anger. I saw that I not only needed to work through my identification with negative emotions, but my identification with positive ones as well.

With this, I suddenly perceived all my desires, strivings, likes, and dislikes as part of an inexorable process of growth. And for a few moments I stood apart, a calm witness of that play of experience. I felt totally at peace.

There are many ways to use anger for growth: trying to find the feelings that underlie my anger, writing in my journal, working through my feelings until I find some self-knowledge. I may even accept my anger as a positive expression of purification, then witness it and let it pass.

The potential benefits of anger are also many: patience, forgiveness, understanding, compassion, and even bliss.

CHAPTER VIII

Blockading Growth

The Gift of Self-Consciousness

And until you own
This: Die and become!
You will be just a dreary guest
On the dark Earth.

—Goethe

This morning while I was writing, Susan walked into our bedroom carrying my socks and slippers and tossed them at my feet. She then declared that even though I thought I was orderly and neat, I only kept my desk organized and left things out of place everywhere else in the house. She did grant that I had improved over a few years ago.

"I'm at least as neat as you," I protested.

Then I took her on a tour of the house, noting that whereas she happened to catch my slippers out of place, her jacket and socks, not to mention a pair of slacks and her purse, had all been left out. I returned to my work. But somehow I could not get my concentration back . . .

Even when I am "right," if I become the least bit defensive, I lose touch with the center of myself and with the center of the stream of our growth together. Actually, that is what happens when I am only slightly defensive. When I really put up my shields, I notice that any sense of a graceful relationship with life dissolves. Then life, and my relationship with Susan, starts to feel empty, or even worse, hateful.

One of the surest ways I have found to lose grace is to become defensive.

Defensiveness is a strange phenomenon. How many times have I defended myself by saying something that in a calmer state would seem ridiculous? I may sense the absurdity of what I am saying, I may even realize that I am only resisting my own growth, yet still not be able to stop myself. Defensive arguing tends to build an irrational momentum all its own.

Then again, defensiveness often expresses a very agile and rational intelligence. When defensive, I may parry every argument; I may turn the tables on Susan and put *her* on the defensive; I may confuse, elude, befog, and incite. Defensiveness can be just deft enough, and just intelligent enough, to make growth all but impossible.

In which case, defensiveness is not so intelligent. When I argue defensively, I blind myself to my faults and resist my own growth. I do not even see what is in my own best interests. I am a bit like a drunk blindly crashing around a dark

room, only instead of upsetting furniture, I over-
turn the possibilities for happiness and growth
in my marriage.

They say man's self-consciousness distinguishes
him from other creatures. Perhaps our self-
consciousness does distinguish us. At least it enables
us to create problems on top of problems, by denying we have a problem.

Within the intimacy and privacy of marriage,
amid all the temptations to dishonesty, lies a wealth
of opportunities for growth. Intelligence is not the
key to making the most of those opportunities.
Intelligence can serve to contract the ego as easily as
expand the ego. Rather, the key lies in self-honesty,
a self-honesty deep enough to touch the core of
our being.

A Subconscious Affair

He who feels punctured
Must once have been a bubble.

—Lao Tsu

Today I was trying to figure out just why I become defensive. I don't claim to be perfect, so why, when under fire, will I passionately deny all fault?

Do I expect Susan to accept that I am without flaw? Do I hope that my denials will somehow raise her opinion of me? If so, then I must be going about it all wrong: when I defend myself, Susan just argues all the harder to prove my fault.

Actually, if I really wanted to raise Susan's opinion of me, instead of defending myself, I would try to see her point of view. I might even thank her for pointing out to me my challenge to grow. (She would probably melt on the spot.) But this goes against the grain of defensiveness. When I am feeling defensive, the last thing I want to do is thank Susan for her insights into my character.

No, defensiveness is not an instinct to gain the love and respect of others, but an instinct to preserve *self*-love and *self*-respect.

Unfortunately, self-love is not a conscious affair. Self-love is an affair of the subconscious, and the subconscious doesn't miss much. When I refuse to acknowledge my need to grow, I imply that my faults are too deep and pervasive to be corrected. When I defensively deny fault, I create a subconscious sense of *irredeemable* fault.

And become all the more defensive.

Ultimately, defensiveness is a self-perpetuating illusion. It perpetuates the illusion that if I give up an illusion about myself (that I am relatively flawless), then I will lose my worthiness as a human being; I will become less. And this illusion traps me into feeling that I am less.

There is only one door out of this trap: face my need to grow.

When I face my need to grow, I begin to see myself from the outside as well as from the inside. This is not a loss, but an expansion of self. If I feel smaller, it is because I have gained a bigger perspective on myself. This bigger perspective may hurt initially (like coming into the light when you have been in a dark room for your whole life), but it holds possibilities for self-love far deeper than the fragile self-love preserved by denying fault.

The subconscious mind keeps us honest, for true self-love demands good reason. Facing our need to grow is the first step toward finding that reason.

When all is said and done, intimacy demands that we face the pain of our shortcomings; to come closer to each other, our egos have to soften.

Only as we open to our challenges to grow can we open ourselves to life and to others.

Fallen Facts

Whoever does not receive the kingdom of God as a little child, shall not enter it.

—Mark 10:15

Yesterday we had a minor scuffle. It went something like this:

SUSAN. Why don't we take some time together this weekend? You're always working. You never want to be with me.

HENRY. What are you talking about? A few weeks ago we went out to dinner together. We're going to your parents' this Wednesday. And I was planning to take a walk with you this afternoon. You're making a fuss about nothing.

When I become defensive, the first thing I am apt to do is cite fact after fact to prove my innocence. This fact in itself proves I am far from the truth.

As far as growing through our relationship goes, truth and fact are not always the same thing. They may even entirely oppose each other.

Facts can be used defensively to create self-serving half-truths. When we defensively cite facts, we dislocate ourselves from our integrity, our center, our love for each other. When we are open to discovering the truth, we do not lose touch with ourselves, even though working through our disagreements. Instead of becoming agitated and alienated from each other, we remain open to growing, to learning. We may even end up feeling a deeper appreciation for each other and closer as a result.

Truth is not merely factual. Truth is a quality of feeling, of openness, innocence, and integrity. When we connect with this innocent integrity within ourselves, even though ignorant of the facts, we will speak only truth.

Do I want to be true when I am with Susan? Then what counts is the quality of my feelings: Do I feel innocent and vulnerable? Do I care about her feelings? Am I open to her point of view? Or do I feel agitated, defensive, and constricted?

Finding truth may require letting go of facts that seem true, facts like "just last week we went out to dinner together," for if those facts allow me to resist growing, then they are not true. They will neither serve my happiness, nor our happiness together.

It is easy to accumulate facts, but truth is only found on the arduous path of knowing oneself.

Sometimes the best I can do when feeling defensive is to not say a word and simply resist the temptation to cite facts. I may not be able to immediately drop my defensiveness, but at least I can stop arguing on its behalf.

Gradually we are beginning to trust each other to be true as opposed to factual. Love requires this trust.

Dark Night of Growth

In heaven above,
And earth below, they best can serve true gladness
Who meet most feelingly the calls of sadness.
                                            —William Wordsworth

Sometimes overcoming defensiveness and facing the challenge to grow can open the door to a different kind of pain.

In the first several years of our marriage, Susan regularly confronted me for being self-centered and selfish. Yet I always managed to deflect her criticisms (to me, they never seemed pertinent). Finally, one time she hinted that she was not the only one bothered by my selfishness. When I pressed further, she claimed that our friends had also observed it. She said that some had even commented on it to her.

First I denied it, then I felt the unfairness of it; finally I managed to admit to it—and felt totally miserable.

Since then, this has happened a number of times: Susan calls me on something; I resist my defensiveness; I admit she is right—only to feel oppressed instead of released. Not that I think I am a terrible person. I just feel an amorphous hopelessness. The clean sword of pain that is supposed to liberate turns out to be more like a hammer pounding me to the ground.

Over the years I have come to realize that at such times it is useless to lament the loss of my happiness, for the more I resent my depression, the more hopeless I become. Yet when I accept my depression as part of the process of growth, I suddenly feel less depressed.

Wisdom lies in embracing the process of growth, with all its peaks and valleys.

I have also noticed that when caught by depression, it helps to give as much as I can to those around me. Giving proves that depression does not have the last word.

Perhaps depression is not so much an alienation from grace as it is the purgative side of grace. Depression may be only the natural backlash of having rejected, time and again, the pain that could have located me in the center of meaning in my life. In which case, if I face my depression now, I can still find that center of meaning.

Deadly Sympathy

You should run a thousand miles from such expressions as: "I was right." "They had no reason for doing this to me." "The one who did this to me was wrong." God deliver us from this poor way of reasoning.
—St. Teresa of Avila

In the first several years of our marriage, when Susan and I were going through rough times, I occasionally shared with a few close friends some of my marital woes. Good friends that they were, they often assured me that I was in the right and Susan in the wrong. One even encouraged me to pursue a relationship with another woman who was attracted to me.

Needless to say, such reassurances were wonderfully uplifting. I began to realize that I had practically been a saint all along.

As the saying goes, with friends like these . . .

Friends offering well-meaning sympathy are found readily; even the most casual acquaintance may offer that much. But it is a rare friend who can help us face our challenges to grow and yet remain a friend. I can only think of one friend I have like that: Susan.

Let Your Partner Be Your Advisor

Recently, we seem to have taken ten steps backward in our relationship. I am not even sure why, but we have been arguing more, and usually about the most picayune things. Last night it came to a head. We were arguing about who was keeping who up at night. Susan claimed that my reading kept her up.

"No way," I insisted, "I only read until you come upstairs. Then I always start getting ready for bed."

"But I'd come upstairs sooner if you weren't busy reading," replied Susan. "Besides, you never stop reading when I come up."

"Oh, don't give me that."

About this time the dam broke, and Susan heatedly listed a myriad of ways I had wronged her over the past month. Not only was I keeping her up at night, but I was putting her down and not helping her around the house.

Perhaps I was just tired, perhaps I'd had my fill of bickering; whatever it was, I just had no strength left to deny her accusations. Instead, I did something I had never done in the midst of an argument: I asked for her advice.

"Susan," I said with full sincerity, "if you were my most trusted advisor, and I promised to do whatever you thought best for me and for our relationship, what would you advise me to do?"

Susan became quiet. She had hardly expected this. For a full half-minute she searched for a response that would warrant this sudden show of trust. Finally, she tactfully described how some of the things I had said and done lately had made her feel. As it turned out, her barrage of criticisms boiled down to a few completely understandable complaints.

Within minutes we had agreed on steps I should take, not only to satisfy her, but to become a better husband, father, and human being. I wanted to take these steps as much as she wanted me to take them. We ended up feeling closer than we had in weeks.

Why shouldn't Susan be my most trusted advisor? I often think I can wisely guide her, why not allow her to guide me? I would probably have to pay a professional therapist for months just so he could come to know me half as well. All Susan costs me is the effort to get my ego out of the way.

CHAPTER IX

The Path of Personal Sex

Personal Versus Impersonal Sex

Erotic love, if it is love, has one premise. That I love from the essence of my being—and experience the other person in the essence of his or her being.

—Erich Fromm

Last night we made love. It was not wild and passionate; actually, it was very calm. Yet we really felt our love for each other, and not simply because we were feeling good. It was not just "great sex." We *made love*.

I have heard that improving sex in a relationship begins by improving the relationship during the rest of the day. Communicating, giving, and expressing love in various ways throughout the day is said to be good foreplay. I am sure that this is true. But what about during sex? Shouldn't we also connect in our love for each other then?

I used to take it for granted that this would happen whenever we had sex, as if all we had to do was enjoy each other, and our love would take care of itself. Yet growing in love means giving. It means dying to what is small, selfish, and inappropriate within ourselves. And that rarely takes care of itself.

When we see sex as a recreational activity—as a break from growing together—then instead of a union of love, sex can become subtly impersonal. It can become an isolated activity, distinct from tenderness, love, and caring for each other. Not only may such impersonal sex fail to bring us closer, but we may even feel let down and irritated afterward. Susan and I have even found ourselves arguing afterward (either about our lovemaking or about something totally unrelated).

Unfortunately, when pleasure is the object of our sex, we can begin to perceive *each other* as objects and miss out on the pleasure of love.

Something very different happens, however, when we embrace the beauty, depth, and mystery of each other as whole persons, as well as each other's bodies. Then sex becomes a personal union, wherein connecting in love is the goal. Such personal sex *is* making love. It leaves us fulfilled in a richness of love. And I have yet to see it end in argument.

Sex is so much more satisfying when we bring all of ourselves to the bedroom. For we are more than sexual beings, even during sex.

The Art of Making Love

Love can inspire the wish for sexual union; in this case the physical relationship is lacking in greediness, in a wish to conquer or to be conquered, but is blended with tenderness.

—Erich Fromm

Lately, I am discovering that there is a vast difference between wanting Susan and loving Susan. For one thing, wanting her demands sex for satisfaction; loving her is fulfilling in itself.

The best lovemaking is the play of this fulfillment.

Making love in the truest sense is not just having sex, but being together. It is enjoying each other's company, holding each other, looking into each other's eyes, and sharing our thoughts, experiences, and feelings. It is also forgetting most of what we normally do leading up to, during, and after impersonal sex.

When making love, we can forget about trying to get each other into the mood; we can forget about trying to have fantastic orgasms; we can forget about trying to climax at the same time. These things are entirely superfluous. We need only connect as two human beings in love—and then stay that way.

Actually, sex may not even be a part of this connection, but if it is, then it will happen naturally, without hurry and without a specific goal in mind. If we decide not to have sex, so long as we have connected more deeply, we still will have made love.

And yes, making love also means playfulness, going with bursts of passion, moving with each other to enhance our pleasure. Still, we can remain connected in our hearts. Sex should heighten our love, not replace our love.

First Deserve, Then Desire

As the soft yield of water cleaves obstinate stone,
So to yield with life solves the insoluble.

—Lao Tsu

For years I have noticed that when Susan loses interest in making love, if I press the issue, we just end up arguing. No wonder. Pressing the issue when Susan is not interested shows that it is not love, but my own pleasure I am after.

Lately, though, I am noticing that Susan's interest rekindles spontaneously—once I stop pushing for sex and put my attention on giving.

Forget about stimulating each other. Stimulate love and have patience. The rest follows naturally.

Providential Passion

This morning I realized how much the creative feeling between a man and a woman finds its source in sexual vitality, in passion. A pure experience of passion can open our eyes to the depths of each other like almost nothing else can.

That is what happened this morning. I saw within Susan a womanliness so rich, springing from a source of beauty so deep, that I felt humbled. I saw not only her beauty as a woman, but what I can only describe as her *divine womanliness.* I saw (not merely believed) that she is made in the image of God.

In various cultures God has been conceived as both male and female. Our passion can show us the truth of both conceptions.

Lead into Gold

Abstinence sows sand all over
The ruddy limbs & flaming hair,
But Desire Gratified
Plants fruits of life and beauty there.
—William Blake

It occurs to me that in itself, passion is neither good nor bad, neither truly creative nor destructive, neither loving nor lustful. Passion transcends polarities. Passion is pure energy, aliveness, and like life itself, it starts off neutral; it is a given. We are the ones that give the energy of passion direction and meaning. Passion can either distract us from love or empower our love.

Passion focused on body parts, to the exclusion of intimately connecting with each other as whole persons, distracts us from love. Instead of drawing us closer, such passion exaggerates the distance between us by creating a fascination with each other as objects, as bodies. Yet when we focus our passion on each other as persons, then passion becomes the catalyst for taking us higher. It vitalizes our love. It allows us to touch levels of feeling and intimacy that we could never experience by denying our passion.

In the early days of our relationship, Susan and I had little discrimination regarding our passion. We would start off feeling our love for each other, then hop into bed and instantly switch gears into just "having sex."

Yet even then we knew that it was not love we were acting on, and afterward we often felt let down and empty. So we would say to ourselves, "All right, we've experienced that. We've satisfied that desire. Now let's move on." But inevitably, the next time we would make the same mistake, and afterward, feel the same emptiness.

Finally, we realized that passion channeled in the direction of lust can never be fulfilled. Lust is self-perpetuating, not an organic desire of the whole person, but a compulsion sidetracking our desire for intimacy and love. We realized that there is only one way to fulfill passion: channel it into love.

Yet passion will not be channeled into love by force. It has to happen naturally: when all we feel is sexual desire, instead of closing our eyes and jumping in, instead of playing the ascetics and trying to ignore our desire, we need only surround our physical desire with our desire for intimacy and love. We already want to feel an intimate connection and to grow in our love. The secret lies in bringing our passion into the context of *that* desire.

Growth does not mean killing desire, but rather, allowing desire to evolve.

The more we have succeeded in channeling passion into love, the more attractive we have become to each other, and the more attractive our relationship has become to both of us.

Spiritual growth can be an aphrodisiac too.

Magnetic Integrity

I admit, last night I was more interested in Susan's body than in her. But Susan was more drawn to an intimate, loving connection.

There was a time when we had an unspoken rule to cover such situations: The one who wanted sex came first, the one who wanted love had to wait. Yet over the years we noticed that this approach often created subtle resentment. Not only that, the more we followed this rule, the more an evolving sexual relationship began to feel like an impossible ideal. Eventually, we realized that we would never grow by seducing each other into old, familiar patterns. Growing together means taking responsibility for each other.

So last night, instead of giving in to my desire, Susan took the lead. She did not push me away. She did not accuse me of wanting something other than love. She looked into my eyes and told me that she loved me. She talked about her day. She asked me about mine. We did make love, but by that time, we were connected enough that it was love we made.

Like a magnet, love in one has the power to draw out love in the other.

I also remember times when the tables have been turned, and Susan was the one with the amorous appetite. On occasion, I even felt irritated by her desires. I remember thinking, "She's just not as interested in growing as I am." I even wondered how long our relationship could last, because I did not want to sacrifice my integrity as a spiritual seeker.

Now I know better. If I am self-righteous or judgmental in refusing Susan's desire then no need to worry: I don't have much integrity to sacrifice.

When I become judgmental of Susan, I need only recall how many times she has been the one desiring to connect in our hearts. Even if in this moment I am more interested in love, our roles could easily be reversed next week, tomorrow, or the next minute.

More important than not indulging each other's physical desire is not indulging any taint of self-righteousness.

Ideally, in marital sex there should be no need for refusal—just a gentle, silent redirecting that leads both partners toward the charm of love.

Shameful Guilt

We cannot well do without our sins; they are the highway of our virtue.

—Thoreau

The other day I read an article that encouraged enjoying all of one's sexual impulses without inhibition, guilt, or shame.

I agree: understanding that our sexual impulses are normal is important. Yet feeling shame can be equally important, especially when we make love in a way that has nothing to do with love.

What is shame but our natural desire for more, letting us know when we have gone for less? Shame is a natural form of self-correction. It prods us to follow our higher instincts, to move toward more love, more true intimacy, more true happiness. Shame helps keep our growth on course. Without shame, we could indulge shamelessly. I doubt if we would have gotten anywhere on the path of personal sex without it.

The self-reproach of guilt, however, often is opposed to growth. Whereas shame implies that I am more than what I have done, guilt implies that I am less for what I have done. Shame cleanses and uplifts; guilt stomps on self-esteem.

Another thing I have noticed about guilt: when I am feeling guilty, I tend to make extreme resolutions to "never do that again." This immediately makes me feel better, but I usually end up doing the same thing again and again anyway.

The habit of making extreme resolutions out of guilt is itself a vice; it allows me to avoid the pain that can change me.

We cannot jump over, in one leap, all the territory through which we must travel to learn to love, no matter how resolved we may be. We need to patiently traverse that territory, take in all its detail, and face all the dangers and mystery there.

Rather than indulge in guilt, we can simply feel the pain of our mistakes, and let that pain pass. Rather than dwell on our mistakes, we can dwell on our desire to love more. Rather than make absolute resolves, we can make a more modest resolve: to do our best to give love a chance next time.

Why dwell in guilt when mistakes are a part of growing? Striving for love is enough. Our bodies are for learning lessons.

Actually, the difference between shame and guilt may only be a matter of a different subconscious interpretation of the same pain, the pain of having made a mistake. In which case, the best way to deal with guilt may be to consciously reinterpret it as shame: "Making a mistake does not mean I am a bad person. I am not condemned. Mistakes are an inevitable part of growing. This pain exists to guide me; it is a gift."

Getting the distorted pain of guilt to settle into the natural pain of shame is an important step of growth. True contrition, it is said, can bring one closer to God than if one never erred at all.

Supersensuous Love

After last night, I am convinced that the greatest pleasure during sex comes when we place the least emphasis on getting pleasure.

Susan and I were making love. We felt very connected. We were talking and now and then just moving playfully; we were not looking for thrills, we were just being together. Then at one point I began to feel as if my whole being was flowing into her. This feeling became more and more intense, until we melted into each other in the most sublime, love-filled orgasm. We came together. But not physically.

I was not sure what had happened. I told Susan that I had just had a "spiritual orgasm." She said that it had happened to her too. We continued to make love, and a moment later it happened again, then again and again. Each time it started in our hearts—a loving energy gathering intensity—until that love peaked and blissfully rushed throughout our bodies. We even distinctly felt a subtle, blissful energy flowing back and forth between us.

There seemed to be no limit as to how long we could go on, but after a short time we went back to simply being together. They may have been the most sublime orgasms we'd ever had, but we did not want to make them the king of our lovemaking.

Even spiritual orgasms emanating from our hearts, if we place them higher than our love, will take us out of our love. And off the path of personal sex.

No single experience, no matter how sublime or satisfying, can be a touchstone for successful lovemaking. The only touchstone for that is the love ignited in our hearts.

Conservation Crazy?

After our "supersensuous lovemaking" a few nights ago, I realized what had made that experience possible. Making love without an orgasm (*coitus interruptus*) may seem idiosyncratic and out of place in a modern marriage, yet if any one thing has helped us discover the path of personal sex, it has been just that. In fact, far more often than not, we make love with the intention *not* to have an orgasm.

This is not a technique we learned somewhere. It has evolved naturally, not only as our sole method of birth control, but out of our personal spiritual practices and our desire to stay connected in our hearts. We have found that making love without the expectation of an orgasm eliminates a subtle level of self-absorption in our sex. We can simply enjoy each other. We can also make love for as long as we want without straying from our love. And so long as we keep the emphasis on connecting in our hearts, making love in this way is not only easy, but totally fulfilling.

Besides, sex that has orgasm as its object is not personal sex. If one or both of us is to have an orgasm, it will happen naturally, when that is our desire. Personal sex may or may not culminate in an orgasm. Either way, connecting in our hearts

171

as two whole human beings is far richer and more satisfying than just going for an orgasm could ever be.

Personal sex is proof that love itself is the most sublime experience.

In a sense, personal sex may be to a married couple what celibacy is to a monk or nun, for both spiritualize sexual energy, both channel passion into love. This also means that we must have some energy left to spiritualize.

Sexual Technique

Eros . . . takes wings from human imagination and is forever transcending all techniques, giving the laugh to all the "how to" books by gaily swinging into orbit above our mechanical rules, making love rather than manipulating organs.

—Rollo May

This afternoon my friend Michael enthusiastically suggested I read a book on Tantric sex. He said that he and his wife Joanne were discovering how to prolong sexual pleasure and "convert sexual into spiritual energy." He described the technique he was learning, which involved thrusting a prescribed number of times (while counting), then pausing, then repeating the procedure.

I told him that we already had a technique for converting sexual into spiritual energy and enhancing pleasure: our love.

No doubt the sexual techniques described in numerous books have helped many couples enjoy a more satisfying sex life. Yet if anything runs the risk of making sex an activity in itself, instead of an expression of love, it is approaching sex as technique.

One of the big problems with sexual techniques is that they tend to abstract experience from its natural setting. For instance, in talking with Michael, I gathered that his impression of Tantric sex was one of couples in torrid embrace for hours on end, the man with superhuman sexual prowess giving the woman the experience of her life. Yet for all we know, this conception could be far from the original intent of Tantra. More importantly, in trying for this conception of a peak experience, a couple is likely to lose touch with the immediacy of their love. It is this immediacy that could lead them to their own natural peak experience.

Experiences of supersensuous love spontaneously occur on the path of personal sex; take them out of their personal and spiritual context (the context in which they naturally occur), and they too will sound exotic and tantalizing—and lose all meaning.

Techniques only attempt to systematize what was originally someone's spontaneous experience. Rather than follow the lead of someone else's experience and entrust our love life to techniques, why not be pioneers, and trust in our own ability to follow the charm of love?

The best sex happens through sensitivity, giving, innocence, and love. Transform even these into techniques and we invite something less than love.

Even in a dark room, everything is there; to see, we only have to turn on the light. To travel the path of personal sex, we do not need techniques. We need only turn on the light—of our love, discrimination, honesty, and desire to grow—in the bedroom. Then have the courage to trust in our own personal experience over everything we have ever learned about sex.

Fast Sex and Sex Fasts

Last night we broke a fast of several weeks. A sex fast, that is. And while making love, we both experienced a particular quality of bliss that we had felt only once before: six and a half years ago, when we conceived Gemma. This time there was not only that bliss, but a delicacy of love and a tenderness that we have rarely touched before.

Fasting from sex for extended periods is something we have found ourselves spontaneously drawn to over the years. In some respects, the benefits are similar to those of fasting from food.

Anyone who fasts regularly (from food) knows that fasting can be an experience not only of purification, but of resetting one's entire approach to eating. Fasting can attune one to the hidden subtleties of eating. Subtleties such as: Am I scarfing my food? Am I bothering to chew? Should I really be eating this? And after the fast, tastes that one previously took for granted become exquisite. An avocado sandwich is suddenly cause for ecstasy, a blueberry cheesecake, nothing short of ambrosial.

Likewise, fasting from sex has at times helped purify and reset our entire physical relationship—especially when we have seen our fast, not as a period of denial, but as a time for connecting exclusively in our hearts. Then a sex fast gives us the chance to drop old patterns of relating, to grow beyond our physical needs and desires. We get the chance to rediscover a sense of self-sufficiency and then to rediscover a fresh intimacy.

Coming off our sex fast last night, we wondered why this lovemaking felt so special. We sensed a tangible magic in the air, as if everything in the room was subtly changing, becoming softer, reflecting our love. Our whole world seemed to be changing. Suddenly we both realized that we had conceived.

We were so certain of this that today at work I called my sister Chris to break the news.

"Hi, Chris. Guess what?"

"What?"

"Susan's pregnant."

"You're kidding!"

"Nope."

"Really? That's great! Have you told mom and dad yet?"

"Well, no, not yet."

"When did you find out?"

"Just last night."

"So Susan did the test, and it was positive?"

"Well, no. Actually we just conceived last night."

Doubt-laden silence suddenly filled the phone lines. "So Susan hasn't even had the test yet?" Chris asked slowly.

"No. I think you have to wait a month or so to do the test. But don't worry," I added quickly, "we'll do it."

"Well, let me know how it turns out. And, uh, maybe you should wait to tell mom and dad."

"You're probably right. Thanks, Chris."

That was good advice. We did not tell anyone else until the test results were in—positive.

Beyond Personal Sex

Chastity is a wealth that comes from abundance of love.
—Rabindranath Tagore

A few nights ago we made love. We felt our love, we felt connected in our hearts, and perhaps just for this reason we both realized something more clearly than we ever have before: sexual desire in itself has little to do with love.

We both saw that sex, no matter how personal, will always contain an element of attachment that is quite apart from love in its motivation. This is not to say that we should have taken a vow of celibacy the day we married. Learning to make love with love has offered one of the greatest areas for growth in our relationship. It has also joined us in a union of love that I doubt could have been created otherwise. Yet even the path of personal sex is but a path, and a path is not an end in itself; hopefully it leads somewhere.

So for a while we talked about what we were feeling. Finally, Susan came up with an analogy. She said that for her, personal sex is like a bridge: one leading from the infatuation of romance, to the selflessness of mature love.

This rang true to me. After all, we cannot jump over all our needs and desires that obstruct selfless love. But we can divert those needs and desires into a more personal expression. We can create a bridge to cross over self-centered needs and desires, by personalizing, and then fulfilling, our needs and desires.

What, then, lies on the further shore of the bridge of personal sex? Barren disinterest? Harsh asceticism?

No. We cross over this bridge of desire to grow in love beyond desire. We cross over this bridge of desire to reach love that is Love.

CHAPTER X

Final Note

Memories over Crepes

It is impossible to reckon how much a husband owes a wife or a wife a husband. It is an infinite debt, it can be paid only in eternity.

—Goethe

At a small French restaurant near the shores of Lake Washington in Seattle, on a full moon night over twelve years ago, I asked Susan to marry me. I do not clearly remember that night, but I do remember the dreams we shared: happiness, success, enlightenment—we would have them all. They were worthwhile dreams, lofty dreams, uncomplicated dreams . . .

Then last night we went out to dinner to celebrate our twelfth anniversary, this time at a French restaurant near the shores of Puget Sound. It was not as fancy as the restaurant on Lake Washington, but that one had closed, and the food at this one was the best French cuisine we had tasted.

Over dinner we reminisced about our years together. Our path had been so much less spectacular than we had expected—no stellar success or enlightenment as of yet—but we both knew that all we had experienced together was far more real, and far richer, than anything we could have dreamed twelve years ago.

After dinner we took a walk on the beach. It was not a full moon, just a quarter moon. The waves gently lapped the shore, the stars were out, and the air was filled with the luminescence of Being. We talked about how, through all the changes, the conflicts, the love and joys— through everything we had shared—we had been molded and deepened in totally unexpected ways, and united into one.

Then we made our way back to our car. Just as we were getting in, we looked up at the stars one last time. Somehow that night sky—vast, mysterious, and beautiful—seemed to reflect all that had happened to us, and all that was yet to come.

No, we had not fulfilled all our dreams, but ever so gradually, invisibly, our dreams were fulfilling us; that is the way of marriage.

Acknowledgments

This book owes as much to the following people as it does to Susan's and my experience together. My deepest gratitude:

To MMY and MA; anything true and of benefit in this book is but a faint reflection of what they have given us. To Kent Junge, without whose generosity and editorial assistance this book would still be a dream. To our families, for their patience and loving support, and for encouraging us to dream in the first place. To those who offered enthusiasm, encouragement, and editorial advice when it was most needed: Hank and Dolores Borys, Chris Funkhouser, Saroja Strand, Sharon Koch, Jeffrey Ainis, John Welwood, John Clancy, and Bill Howell.

Henry and Susan Borys.
Photo by Lynette Johnson.